Devil's Advocates

DEVIL'S ADVOCATES is a series of books devoted to exploring the classics of horror cinema. Contributors to the series come from the fields of teaching, academia, journalism and fiction, but all have one thing in common: a passion for the horror film and a desire to share it with the widest possible audience.

'The admirable Devil's Advocates series is not only essential – and fun – reading for the serious horror fan but should be set texts on any genre course.'
Dr Ian Hunter, Professor of Film Studies, De Montfort University, Leicester

'Auteur Publishing's new Devil's Advocates critiques on individual titles... offer bracingly fresh perspectives from passionate writers. The series will perfectly complement the BFI archive volumes.' **Christopher Fowler,** *Independent on Sunday*

'Devil's Advocates has proven itself more than capable of producing impassioned, intelligent analyses of genre cinema... quickly becoming the go-to guys for intelligent, easily digestible film criticism.' *Horror Talk.com*

'Auteur Publishing continue the good work of giving serious critical attention to significant horror films.' *Black Static*

DevilsAdvocatesbooks

DevilsAdBooks

ALSO AVAILABLE IN THIS SERIES

Antichrist Amy Simmons

Black Sunday Martyn Conterio

The Blair Witch Project Peter Turner

Candyman Jon Towlson

Cannibal Holocaust Calum Waddell

Carrie Neil Mitchell

The Company of Wolves James Gracey

The Curse of Frankenstein Marcus K. Harmes

Dead of Night Jez Conolly & David Bates

The Descent James Marriot

Don't Look Now Jessica Gildersleeve

The Fly Emma Westwood

Frenzy Ian Cooper

Halloween Murray Leeder

House of Usher Evert Jan van Leeuwen

In the Mouth of Madness Michael Blyth

It Follows Joshua Grimm

Ju-on The Grudge Marisa Hayes

Let the Right One In Anne Billson

Macbeth Rebekah Owens

Nosferatu Cristina Massaccesi

Saw Benjamin Poole

Scream Steven West

The Shining Laura Mee

The Silence of the Lambs Barry Forshaw

Suspiria Alexandra Heller-Nicholas

The Texas Chain Saw Massacre James Rose

The Thing Jez Conolly

Twin Peaks: Fire Walk With Me Lindsay Hallam

Witchfinder General Ian Cooper

FORTHCOMING

Blood and Black Lace Roberto Curti

Creepshow Simon Brown

Daughters of Darkness Kat Ellinger

M Samm Deighan

The Mummy Doris V. Sutherland

Shivers Luke Aspell

Devil's Advocates

The Devils

Darren Arnold

Acknowledgments

Thanks to John Atkinson, and to all who provided encouragement.

First published in 2019 by
Auteur, 24 Hartwell Crescent, Leighton Buzzard LU7 1NP
www.auteur.co.uk
Copyright © Auteur 2019

Series design: Nikki Hamlett at Cassels Design
Set by Cassels Design www.casselsdesign.co.uk

All rights reserved. No part of this publication may be reproduced in any material form (including photocopying or storing in any medium by electronic means and whether or not transiently or incidentally to some other use of this publication) without the permission of the copyright owner.

British Library Cataloguing-in-Publication Data
A catalogue record for this book is available from the British Library

ISBN paperback: 978-1-911325-75-8
ISBN ebook: 978-1-911325-76-5

Contents

Introduction 7

Synopsis 13

Chapter 1: Historical Context 17

Chapter 2: Authorship and Adaptation 31

Chapter 3: Genre 59

Chapter 4: Themes 71

Chapter 5: Gender and Sexuality 81

Chapter 6: Versions and Censorship 89

Chapter 7: Legacy 107

Bibliography 114

This book is dedicated to my son, Alexander.

Introduction

It's very easy to talk—or write—about cinephilia in pre-internet, pre-digital times, but much harder to convey the very specific feelings of frustration which resulted from the practical problems faced by anyone blessed/cursed with the passion during that era. By the time film got its hooks into me, at least the home video market was up and running, providing access way beyond the theatrical (and latterly television) screenings previous generations had been limited to. Not only did possession of a video recorder open up the brave, often lurid new world of the rental market, but it afforded the opportunity for time-shifted viewing. As it happened, neither of those avenues were of much help to me when it came to tracking down the film that's the subject of this book.

The Devils (1971) was a film I'd become intrigued with following a late-night television showing of director Ken Russell's earlier *Women in Love* (1969), which I'd managed to catch some of, albeit not in the clandestine manner I'd hoped for. My parents had seen *The Devils* (separately, due to childcare duties) on its initial theatrical release; my dad enjoyed it, my mum hated it, and, in the film's continued, conspicuous absence in my life, their polarised opinions were virtually the only crumbs of information I had about this tantalising title. If it could attract such radically different views merely within the confines of the family home, what illicit delights could such a film possibly have in store, should I ever be lucky enough to locate it? Oh, and there was also the brief, hardly glowing, yet hugely enticing entry for it in *Halliwell's Film Guide*:

> Despite undeniable technical proficiency this is its writer-director's most outrageously sick film to date, campy, idiosyncratic and in howling bad taste from beginning to end, full of worm-eaten skulls, masturbating nuns, gibbering courtiers, plague sores, rats, and a burning to death before our very eyes. (Halliwell, 1986: 252)

What's not to like? At least that's what the callow, 80s version of me thought when absorbing Leslie Halliwell's unintentionally galvanising words, and the quest escalated. *Surely* the 1980s home video market, with its penchant for bad taste, sex, nudity and graphic violence, would cheerfully support such a title? The best-stocked video shop in our part of Fife met my hopeful telephone enquiry with an emphatic 'No!' without checking—or even pretending to check—their catalogue, and I did of course scour every local petrol station and corner shop which boasted a rack of video tapes; those who remember such video rental methods will confirm that the oddest of titles could pop up anywhere among the expected mainstream releases (although the chances of such jack-in-the-box happenings radically decreased post-1984. I'll elaborate in a moment). I didn't even know if the film had ever been issued on home video—do remember, back then we didn't have Google. Nowadays, you could probably search for, find and begin streaming the film online in the time it's taken you to read this far.

As the 1980s wore on, I headed south across the Forth to study in Edinburgh, where my highly undemanding schedule allowed me to spend plenty of time perusing video stores; by this stage I'd resignedly concluded that the film was not to be had on rickety old VHS (and certainly wasn't going to show up on four-channel TV at any point), and I boxed the film away in my head, labelling it a *film maudit* (or rather, I would have, had I known the term at that point in my life). Optimism was briefly renewed when I chanced upon an ex-rental Warner Bros. tape of Russell's *Lisztomania* (1975), which I duly purchased for £2.99, but any hope that *The Devils* could be similarly rescued from the Stygian depths soon flickered out, and the trail went cold again.

It does now appear that a similar Warners cassette existed of *The Devils* (more details in chapter 6), but doubtless was removed from most shelves following the Video Recordings Act (VRA) of 1984. The VRA was largely introduced to combat the well-documented 'video nasties' phenomenon (which, incidentally, *The Devils* was never associated with), and its effect was to bring the UK's previously, wonderfully unregulated home video market into line with cinema—therefore each and every feature film, no matter how innocuous, needed a British Board of Film Classification (BBFC) certificate. Any given film was faced with two choices: get classified or be pulled from the market, with heavy penalties in place for non-compliance. *The Exorcist* (1973), a film Warner Bros. have always seemed very proud of, was a notable casualty of the VRA, and was finally granted a certificate in the late 1990s.

The costs incurred in submitting a film for classification were not inconsiderable, and it's clear to see why many small distributors found the outlay to be prohibitive: in the year following the VRA's introduction, the price charged by the BBFC to examine a title for video release was £4.60 (plus tax) per minute of film (Kerekes and Slater, 2000: 60).

At the time of writing, submitting a 90-minute film for a DVD/Blu-ray certificate would cost £755.23 inclusive of tax. While many films were submitted for classification, others ended up in fire sales as retailers sought to offload titles which would soon be rendered worthless—although some unscrupulous dealers kept uncertified tapes and simply furnished them with wonkily-applied stickers signifying a rating. The huge backlog of viewing material meant exponential growth for both the BBFC's income and its staffing requirements; the board's number of employees more than quadrupled during the VRA's incipient stages (ibid.).

While Warner Bros., of all distributors, would hardly be financially stretched when it came to the fairly hefty classification costs incurred in the post-VRA market, it seems likely that they were fairly happy for a film they'd never been too comfortable with to be quietly swept away alongside countless other titles from smaller, less moneyed distributors. Whether it was due to Warners' indifference or active dislike, the net result was the same. Meanwhile, back at the ranch, I was unwittingly hunting for a tape of *The Devils* in a void which existed between the VRA's introduction and the day Warners would eventually submit the film, in video form, for classification.

When not combing the racks of Edinburgh's video stores, I spent many hours in the dark of the city's many cinemas, and scanned the film listings in the *Evening News* on a daily basis; while most UK cinemas, then as now, usually changed films on a Friday, there were one or two art-house/repertory establishments which crammed many titles into a single week. One Friday (as I recall, at least), I found a listing for a double bill—due to take place the following day at the Filmhouse on Lothian Road—of Derek Jarman's *Jubilee* (1978) supported by *The Devils*; even then, while panicking that this seemed a bit too good to be true, I instantly spotted the thematic connection (Jarman directed *Jubilee* and designed the sets for *The Devils*), which I felt made the whole affair a lot more credible. The next day, I rose at an hour that was unusually early for students in general and myself in particular, and headed down to the box office to snare a ticket for this particular late-night double feature. No student discount was available, plus it meant I'd get home at around three o'clock in the morning *and* would have to sit through a film I wasn't particularly bothered about (my interest in some of Jarman's films came a bit later, after processing his staggering work on *The Devils*), but no small detail was going to faze me now.

Naturally, I returned to the cinema in good time that evening—at an hour when most right-thinking folk would be heading to bed—and took my seat in the back row. Rather surprisingly, what I had expected to be *Jubilee* opened with the Warner Bros. logo, and I soon realised that the film I'd waited so long to see was about to unfold.[1] I had to quickly reconfigure my brain for this, as I was basically ready to mark time for the best part of a couple of hours while building up to *The Devils*, but for this much younger, more adaptable version of myself, this presented no great problem. The film played and I sat transfixed as it met, and quickly exceeded, any and all expectations that I had. When it finished, I wondered if I'd ever get the chance to see the film again, but nonetheless considered this to be mission accomplished. Anyway, deciding that this experience couldn't be topped by anything Derek Jarman could serve up—and being very pleasantly surprised by the running order—I decided to give *Jubilee* a miss and left the cinema. On the way home I stopped off at the Cameo cinema to take in the second film in their late night double bill, *Blue Velvet* (1986), thereby catching up with a friend I'd originally planned to go to the Cameo with that night, changing arrangements once I learned of the screening of *The Devils*. (Sometime later I also bailed on plans to watch *Pet Sematary* [1989]—a film I still haven't seen—with the same friend, opting to see the much-hyped *Heathers* [1988] instead. Evidently I'm not a good person to make cinema plans with.)

While my friend hated David Lynch's masterpiece (he'd enjoyed the first film, student mainstay *Betty Blue* [1986], which I'd already seen), I found myself in the position of seeing two films which made, and continue to make, a huge impact on me, within the space of a few hours. While the wonders of *Blue Velvet* can't be discussed in detail here, both Lynch's film and *The Devils* see redemption achieved amidst the most nightmarish of circumstances; I didn't make this connection at the time, reeling as I was from the force of this personalised double bill. As memory has it, I saw the original UK theatrical cut of *The Devils* that night, although by the time we get to chapter 6 we'll discover that the odds are against that being the case—which I guess marks me out as an unreliable narrator. Still, that's how I remember it.

Undoubtedly the most notorious title in Ken Russell's filmography—a list which includes numerous other controversial works such as *Women in Love*, *Lisztomania* and *Crimes of Passion* (1984)—*The Devils* caused a genuine furore on its initial theatrical release, only to largely disappear for many years. The 1970s proved to be a prolific period for Russell, but the decade closed with both the aforementioned advent of home video and his slide in reputational and commercial terms, meaning reduced demand was in place for audiences to (re)discover Russell's earlier work via the new small-screen format. As the 1980s reached their latter stages, Russell would actually find an ally in the video market, as his deal with Vestron Pictures was clearly an arrangement in which most eyes were on how the productions would fare as rental titles.[2] While each of these later films received a theatrical release, the brevity of their runs meant that you did quite well if you caught any of Russell's Vestron efforts in a cinema before they sped their way to VHS.

Russell's output in the 1980s was largely dismissed by audiences and critics alike, while the following decade saw the director turn out a series of boilerplate TV movies—although an anomaly was present in the form of his final theatrical feature, *Whore* (1991), released just 20 years after the heady days of *The Devils*. Little was done in the way of seriously reappraising his body of work until the early 2000s (by which time both the internet and DVD were firmly established), when his TV films on composers Delius and Elgar were released on DVD and work on a director's cut of *The Devils* began. While this didn't immediately bring about that much interest in Russell's other films, it did prove to be the starting point for *The Devils* in regaining the recognition which had been absent for the best part of three decades—a recognition which culminated in 2012 with the British Film Institute (BFI) DVD release. It's a film which provides plenty of material for analysis and discussion, and while this has always been the case, it's now especially timely given the exposure and acclaim the film has received in recent years.

Following the upcoming synopsis, this monograph will devote a chapter to the film's historical context, as the timing of the first appearance of *The Devils* is of great importance in a way which spreads out way beyond the confines of the cinema screen. The next chapter will examine the film in terms of authorship and adaptation; as well as having Ken Russell's fingerprints all over it, there are two important source texts which contribute much to the film's genetic makeup. Following that, we have a chapter on genre, as pigeonholing the film is not an especially straightforward task—although had it been available, 1980s video stores would almost certainly have filed it under horror.

Chapter 4 takes a look at the themes prevalent in the film—this is the only film of Russell's which the director considered to be political, and there are other thematic aspects to consider in the rich, dark story. A look at gender and sexuality in the film follows, and discussion of the former can't simply be limited to male/female, as the very first character we see in the film—King Louis XIII—gives us something to think about in terms of gender fluidity; the film also sees perennial sparring partners sex and religion clash to interesting effect. The penultimate chapter looks at the film's censorship travails and the various versions of *The Devils* which have appeared on both big and small screens, and the final chapter is devoted to the film's legacy and influence.

From here on in, unless otherwise stated, the version of *The Devils* being discussed is the composite cut which features two scenes not included in any official home video release. More information on this can be found in chapter 6.

FOOTNOTES

1. Further investigations revealed, for reasons I'm still unclear of, an unusual quirk in that the Filmhouse always showed late-night double bills in reverse order to that advertised, so it turned out it wasn't the projection booth (or programming) mix-up I'd assumed it to be.
2. Vestron had distributed Russell's *Gothic* (1986) in the US, and the film had been a hit for them, particularly when it came to the home video release (Russell, 1989: 274). The success of this venture led to a deal with Russell for three more pictures: *Salome's Last Dance* (1988), *The Lair of the White Worm* (1988) and *The Rainbow* (1989).

Synopsis

Cardinal Richelieu is unimpressed with Louis' performance.

France, the seventeenth century. Cardinal Richelieu, fearful of Huguenot uprisings, is determined to centralise power in the country by stripping cities of their autonomy. One such city, Loudun, is targeted for defortification, but the move is blocked by influential secular priest Urbain Grandier, who holds interim powers in the city following the death of Governor Sainte-Marthe. A chronic womaniser, the vainglorious Grandier impregnates and largely abandons Phillipe, the daughter of Trincant, Loudun's magistrate, who himself is subsequently mocked by the priest. While comforting a plague victim on her deathbed and angrily expelling a chemist and a surgeon who are gleefully administering barbaric, supposedly curative methods to the patient, Grandier encounters the woman's daughter, Madeleine, and the two begin a relationship.

Sister Jeanne, the abbess of the local Ursuline convent, entertains wild sexual fantasies about Grandier and invites him to be the order's new confessor. Grandier has secretly married Madeleine, although the ceremony is surveilled by both the chemist and the surgeon Grandier had previously clashed with; Jeanne is distraught when she learns of the marriage through her own nuns. However, she regains some hope when she's informed that the new confessor has arrived, but is crestfallen when it's revealed to be Trincant's cousin, Father Mignon. An embittered Jeanne tells Mignon that Grandier is a servant of Satan who has placed her, and the rest of the convent, under a spell of lewd desire.

Grandier marries Madeleine.

Grandier temporarily leaves the city to seek assurance from King Louis XIII, a carefree, flamboyant monarch who guaranteed Loudun's safety when Sainte-Marthe was alive. Louis is completely uninterested in and bored by politics, and his indifference to state matters makes it easy for Richelieu to assert his influence. In Grandier's absence, Mignon and Baron de Laubardemont—Richelieu's bellicose emissary, who was thwarted in his attempt to demolish Loudun's walls—plot to find evidence of Jeanne's accusations.

Jeanne is subjected to a grotesque public exorcism presided over by Father Barré, a zealous and seemingly unhinged priest recruited by Laubardemont. As the ritual descends into chaos, the nuns try to save Jeanne from her ordeal; Laubardemont orders that they be executed for their insubordination, but Barré intervenes at the last moment and claims the nuns are suffering from the same affliction as Jeanne. He exhorts them to behave in as blasphemous a manner as possible, and a disguised King Louis visits the apparently possessed order, who are now completely hysterical and almost invariably naked.

Highly amused by these chaotic scenes, Louis suggests to Barré that a phial of Christ's own blood might help cure the nuns. An awestruck Barré carefully takes the container from the king, and the nuns are instantly calmed. Louis then opens the box containing the phial, revealing it to be empty. Because of this crucial exposé, the nuns return to their hysterical state and their behaviour grows even more outrageous: a bible is burned, a large church candle is masturbated and fellated, and a life-sized crucifix is ripped from an altar and used as a prop for a series of sexual acts.

Grandier returns and is appalled as he witnesses the chaos for himself, and both he and Madeleine are arrested. A kangaroo court finds Grandier guilty of sorcery, and he's sentenced to death by burning. Before his execution, Grandier is ecclesiastically tortured but refuses to confess to the bogus charges. A remorseful Jeanne attempts suicide, and her subsequent proclamation of Grandier's innocence is dismissed as the work of the evil spirits which inhabit her. A baying crowd—including Trincant, Phillipe and the baby she's now given birth to—witness Grandier being burned alive, with his executioner having failed to get past the flames in order to perform a planned, merciful strangulation. Mignon realises they've executed an innocent man, and is later consigned to an asylum for his perceived ravings.

While the burning is taking place, Laubardemont wastes no time in ordering the destruction of the city walls. Now Jeanne has served her purpose, Laubardemont visits her and speaks of the sad, lonely life which awaits the nun. He leaves her a 'souvenir' in the form of Grandier's charred femur, which Jeanne later masturbates with. As Grandier's ashes are scattered to the four winds, a bedraggled Madeleine is seen walking away from the city and its ruined fortifications.

Chapter 1: Historical Context

Opening in the UK in July 1971 (has there ever been a less appropriate summer movie?), *The Devils* was extremely graphic for its day, shocking audiences who had nonetheless already been prepped, to a degree at least, for a more violent interpretation on historical drama through the likes of *Witchfinder General* (1968) and *The Blood on Satan's Claw* (1971). *The Devils* was sandwiched between two other highly controversial Warner Bros. films, *Performance* (1970) and *A Clockwork Orange* (1971).[1] The fate of the much-delayed *Performance*, which was filmed in 1968 and subjected to no end of studio interference before its all-too-brief run in cinemas (as it happens, the film is far more suited to the early 70s), may have telegraphed some of the problems which would arise between *The Devils* and its American backers.

The trial of Urbain Grandier.

While the makers of both *Performance* and *The Devils* may have had to push to get the distributor to exhibit their films at all, let alone in versions approximating their directors' visions, *A Clockwork Orange*'s director, Stanley Kubrick, requested that Warners actually remove his film from UK distribution.[2] Of these three films, it's quite likely that the casual viewer may well single out Kubrick's film, with its cold portrayal of violence perpetrated on the weak and helpless, as the most extreme title, but Warners never seemed to have any problem with the film or its director, whom they appeared to acquiesce to at every turn. Russell and *Performance*'s co-directors Nicolas Roeg and Donald Cammell, on the other hand, were evidently not held in high esteem by the studio, which does make one wonder exactly why the company were involved with these films in the first place. As Cammell said of *Performance*, '[t]here are a number of people at Warners who hate the film and all it represents' (Buck, 2012: 267). When it came to *The Devils*, Russell may as well have used Donald Cammell's words verbatim, but more on that later. Although its journey from completion to release had been a protracted and torturous one, at least *Performance* had been and gone before the reactionary fires which roasted *The Devils* had been properly stoked. Cammell also noted how his film marked the end of an era, and connected this with Warners' mistreatment of the movie (Buck, 2012: 281).

With the 1960s coming to a bloody close amidst the terror and chaos of the Altamont Free Concert (an event involving *Performance*'s star Mick Jagger) and the Tate–LaBianca murders by the Manson 'family', the early 1970s saw the world become a far more sombre place, with much of the idealism and optimism of the previous decade replaced by caution and anxiety. In terms of cinema, as early as Michael Reeves' *The Sorcerers* (1967)—the second of just three films the director would complete in his short life—indications were that the jig might be up as far as the swinging sixties were concerned (Cooper, 2011: 18). Reeves' final film (*Witchfinder General*) and subsequent death also went firmly against the grain of the purportedly feel-good decade. *The Devils* contains enough in the way of face value horror to send many heading for the exits, but it's actually the implicit messages which are far more troubling, and this pre-Watergate release, set back in the 1600s, presented its audience with a harrowing example of the consequences of corruption at the highest level.

Richelieu (left) and Laubardemont discuss Grandier.

The Devils was, and remains, a violent film. However, for as long as cinema has existed, opponents of such fare have often failed to grasp that screen horror does not operate in the same space as the real-life horror for which it is analogous. In the real world, the slightest hint of violence can be alarming and unsettling in a way which the most extreme horror films cannot come even remotely close to matching, regardless of whether they are viewed in the home or at a cinema. Take the aforementioned *Performance*, which was filmed before but released after the tragic events of Altamont: Donald Cammell felt that his film, with its inherent violence, possessed precognitive qualities which signalled what would develop at Altamont (Buck, 2012: 282). Conversely, Mick Jagger, as star of both *Performance* and the Altamont concert, is unlikely to have ever given much thought to linking the two, as being present at the scene of a real killing has no correlation with make-believe death as enacted on a movie set—no matter how off-kilter *Performance*'s shoot may have been (Buck, 2012: 155–156, 192–196).

Cammell, like most of us, was presumably limited to watching the mayhem of Altamont unfold via the Maysles' documentary *Gimme Shelter* (1970), making him just another viewer behind the safety of the screen—although in 1996 he did prove a thing or two when it came to taking on death, shooting himself in the head and watching in a mirror as his life ebbed away (a cult of personality ensued, and Cammell's demise has now been virtually retconned into *Performance*). *The Devils* actually has a little more in common with *Gimme Shelter*, which sees audience member Meredith Hunter stabbed to death on camera, than it does with *Performance*; even though the audience of Russell's film knows they're not actually watching Urbain Grandier burn to death, they're aware that he did die like this (the film's opening title card makes this clear), which is a far more upsetting idea than anything presented in the fictional, highly stylised, drug-influenced *Performance*.

Although Abraham Zapruder's 8mm film of John F. Kennedy's assassination on November 22, 1963, wouldn't air publicly until 1975, its existence was common knowledge—still images from the film had been published within a week of the event (as a side note, JFK died on the same day as *The Devils*' author Aldous Huxley; Lord Harlech, who oversaw *The Devils* at the BBFC, was a pallbearer at Kennedy's funeral). Following the inadvertent capture on film of the deaths of both JFK and Hunter, it might be argued that audiences' relationships to death on screen, subconsciously or otherwise, were in a state of flux; now it was widely known that genuine deaths had been recorded on film, lines had become somewhat blurred between real-life violence and on-screen entertainment. Previously, it had been assumed that fact and fiction could be reassuringly compartmentalised at will, and UK cinema audiences had been exposed to many years of newsreels playing before the main feature—an arrangement which provided a clear line of demarcation between verity and fabrication.[3]

More troubling as a concept than the Zapruder and Mayles films and their chance findings, however, was the possibility that Charles Manson and his followers purposely filmed the ritual killings of humans and animals (Sanders, 1971: 210–216). There's something of Schrödinger's cat about this, as the films are said to be somewhere out there yet have never been found. It is alleged that the films, along with other bits of Manson Family paraphernalia, are buried out in the vast deserts of California (Sanders, 1971: 187). The status of these sinister films is enhanced by them seeming to simultaneously exist and not exist, which itself serves to confuse the dividing of the factual and the fictional, the real and the imagined. Inevitably, and most unreassuringly, sensationalism crept in:

> The reason why so little is known about 'death films', [*Game* magazine reporter Dean] Anthony explains, is because of fear. The majority of investigators who worked on the Manson case shied away in horror from digging too deeply. A few were convinced that if they asked too many questions their own lives might be in danger. Not Dean Anthony. He has no hesitation in pronouncing snuff films and their high flying clientele to be the real deal. They exist, he states categorically, alas failing to say on what basis he makes the deduction. (Kerekes and Slater, 2016)

Even if such stories are groundless, the idea that people were not only killed on, but possibly *for*, film was another significant way in which to unsettle all those who consumed the moving image. *The Devils*, with Russell's trademark fast and loose melange of historical fact and wild fantasy, served audiences a rather disquieting bridge between true life horrors of long ago and very contemporary problems lurking outside the cinema auditorium. Up until this point, the magic lantern had mainly functioned as a provider of divertissements, to be enjoyed when the hard day was done. All of a sudden, it had grown some sharp, nasty teeth.

This blurring of the lines goes back as far as Russell's early work for the BBC; Russell often clashed with *Monitor*'s editor Huw Wheldon, who not unreasonably wanted Russell to stick to the facts when making documentaries for the BBC arts programme. Wheldon hated the use of actors in documentaries, and Russell's fondness for putting performers in his *Monitor* films led to many a compromise being thrashed out (Russell, 1989: 22). Among Russell's best-known *Monitor* works are *Elgar* (1962) and *The Debussy Film* (1965), the latter of which featured *The Devils*' Oliver Reed and marked a key point in developing the approach Russell would later employ in feature films, including *The Devils*:

> [*The Debussy Film*] is barely a 'documentary' at all insofar as the film unit within the film is an entirely fictional creation (albeit with some parallels to the film that we are watching). Moreover, by exploiting the film-within-a-film device, *The Debussy Film* also circumvents many of the restrictions that had previously constrained Russell's earlier work. (Hill, 2015)

Despite their frequent disagreements, Russell always held Huw Wheldon in very high regard, and credits him with a key role in the director's career path (Russell, 1989: 22). A favourite saying of Wheldon's, 'to make the good popular and the popular good', appears to have at least partially been taken on board by Russell, considering his quest to demystify highbrow material for the wider public. Via his numerous works on artists of various disciplines—films made both under and outside of Wheldon's tutelage—Russell attempted to make elitist subject matter accessible without sacrificing intelligence. By the time he got to *The Devils*, Russell was no longer constrained by editorial requirements and therefore had no need to frame his story with a contrived structure such as that employed for *The Debussy* film.[4] With such filters now conspicuously absent, the discrete work that is Russell's film of *The Devils* provides no clue as to where history ends and fantasy begins (the same can be said of the film's predecessor, *The Music Lovers* [1970]). Interestingly, this charge can also be levelled at the Aldous Huxley work which Russell drew upon, and the classification of Huxley's book as a 'documentary novel' possibly tells you all you need to know about its approach to its subject—more on this in the next chapter.

King Louis (left) is bored rigid by Richelieu.

Despite its firm seventeenth-century setting—and its ongoing relevance—The Devils is very much a film for 1971, and its ideas about spirituality said much about the time in which the film was released (more on this in chapter 4). Uncomfortable parallels could also be made with the Troubles in Northern Ireland; this conflict, for which both politics and religion provided much of the fuel, had been underway for some time when The Devils was released. And with the world only starting to recover from the aforementioned Manson murders, which were deemed to have been committed in order to ignite a race war, the film also served up a scarcely-needed reminder of the case's chief bogeyman in the form of Father Barré, who, much like Charles Manson, is a tiresome longhair who cherry-picks and distorts Christ's teachings to suit his own demented ends. Audiences in 1971 certainly had plenty to think about, and The Devils did not provide an easy evening of escapism. The film had much to say to the audience of its time, and the vexatious nature of its message endures to the present day. As Marc Bridle, in his 2004 review of the same year's restored cut, writes:

> Seventeenth century religious extremism can seem almost identical to twenty-first century religious extremism: the Catholic terror that Richelieu supplants to Loudun is identical to the Islamic terrorism that fundamentalists supplant to Western democracies. Is this partly why, in post 9/11 USA, Russell's The Devils is still viewed as disturbing and unpalatable?

Given that many of the big, and indeed all of the current, problems that the film has encountered regarding distribution have lain with Warner Bros. in the US, Bridle has posited a very interesting theory here; many have presumed that Warners' reluctance and/or belligerence when it comes to *The Devils* is rooted in a need to avoid religious controversy, and while that may well still be the case, Warners' reasoning, in an age after the World Trade Center attacks, may be rather more complex than one might first suspect.

The idea that the film may possess an enduring element and can't be conveniently dismissed as a product of its time is what really hints at the real power of Russell's vision. Father Barré aside (see below), there's nothing in *The Devils* to mark it out as a nostalgia trip for present-day audiences, and it carefully avoids the modish trappings which feature in so many films of the era. Although it has many parallels with *The Devils*, Arthur Miller's 1953 play *The Crucible*, while rightly acknowledged as a classic of twentieth-century theatre, presents a contemporary audience with feelings of distance and security, as the events it explicitly depicts (the Salem witch trials) and implicitly criticises (the House Un-American Activities Committee's investigations) are both safely tucked away in the past. The notion that the thorniness at the heart of *The Devils* has an incredibly long reach and may never cease to have relevance is troubling, for quite different reasons, to both those who stand in favour of the film and those who oppose it.

A little over a year prior to the film's release, the UK had experienced a major shock in the form of a general election result in which incumbent prime minister Harold Wilson's Labour administration, expected to win comfortably, were defeated by Ted Heath's Conservatives.[5] The swing to the right can be partly attributed to a desire to sweep away many of the liberal ideals of the 1960s and the 'permissive society' which had developed during that decade. This sea change in both government and a vocal section of society did not make for an ideal climate for *The Devils*' release (Robertson, 1989: 135). While the film's release and content may have been fodder for all those who argued against permissiveness, *The Devils* does show the sort of damage which can be inflicted by repression, as Sister Jeanne's pent-up fantasies about Grandier eventually boil over to the extent where they cost the priest his life.

The film does contain one notable concession to the period in which it was made, in the form of Father Barré (the final vowel in his name isn't accented in the film's credits, but we'll do right by him here), who is somewhat anachronistic in appearance. While he may share a hairstyle and glasses with the John Lennon of the time, the militant Barré isn't remotely interested in giving peace a chance, and the exorcist's overall look is completely at odds with what come to be established as his trademark ravings. In loosely mirroring Lennon's late Beatles/early solo style, Barré's physical appearance also serves to remind audiences of the breakup of the Beatles—yet another reminder of the way in which the 1960s had turned sour.

Father Barré. To the right we can glimpse Twiggy, who would go on to star in Russell's next film.

While other characters in the film—Richelieu, Laubardemont, and so on—prove to be as severe and devious as they look, the art of physiognomy would fall way short of accurately assessing Barré. He wouldn't look at all out of place in another French-set film of the same year, Jacques Rivette's 13-hour *Out 1* (1971), and could easily pass for a patron of that film's ostensible shop, L'angle du hasard; overlooking the required time travel aspect, it's not much of a stretch to imagine him stumbling out of Rivette's Paris and hitchhiking west to Loudun.[6] Barré stands as virtually the film's sole explicit reference to the early 1970s, and there's little else in the movie (barring the ages of the actors) to date the production.

If we take *The Devils* to be an astute commentary on the void which had opened up as soon as the 1970s arrived, a couple of years after the film's release came the ultimate statement regarding the world's post-1960s malaise in the form of Jean Eustache's *The Mother and the Whore* (*La Maman et La Putain*, 1973). Eustache's shattering masterpiece is, quite simply, one of the greatest films ever made, and has more than one aspect in common with Russell's film. Besides being set in France, *The Mother and the Whore* also features a narcissistic, conceited man-child as its central character, and we watch him flit from one woman to the next until, eventually, even he runs out of steam as he receives news of a pregnancy. But these superficial similarities pale in comparison to the manner in which the film both marks the end of an era and heralds a new, much darker age. Both *The Devils* and *The Mother and the Whore* managed to tap into the sense that a serious fracture had occurred in the world, and while neither offered any alternatives or suggestions of a way forward, the two films nonetheless perfectly captured the zeitgeist of the early 1970s and set out enduring truths. Jonathan Rosenbaum, analysing *The Mother and the Whore*, notes:

> [A] definitive expression of the closing in of Western culture after the end of the era generally known as the 60s. Yet what spooks me about seeing it today is that it looked like the tail end of something back in 1973 and even in the early 80s, but it registers in 1999 like something we're still living inside—a Rip van Winkle slumber that's lasted so long we're all pretty well convinced that it must be reality. What is that something? A terminal collapse of will and hope and a mistrust of freedom that all too often passes for the human condition. (1999)

Rosenbaum could just as easily have been writing about *The Devils*. As per *The Devils*, *The Mother and the Whore* found no shortage of opponents on its initial release, and was condemned by some as being immoral and obscene (this was mainly due to its frank dialogue as opposed to anything that's seen on screen; this perhaps highlights how the parameters for what is considered 'obscene' are so different on each side of the English Channel). The two films share an uncanny ability to unnerve through their very veracity, but Eustache's film, mired in a rights issue presided over by the director's son, remains frustratingly difficult to see—at least via official channels. Even back in the early 1970s, railing against a creative work was not an especially new pastime, and Russell and Eustache had both fashioned films which, on the face of it, were easy to object to, yet digging deeper into the philosophies at work in these films (*The Devils*' turn will roll round in chapter 5), it appears that both films share a very traditionalist core that their detractors may well approve of should they bother to scratch the surface(s). In his review of *The Mother and the Whore*, Richard Brody writes:

> Eustache delivers nothing less than a comprehensive vision of France's post-1968 revolution—and it's a ferociously conservative view. He fills the film's three and a half hours with the loam of collective memory—the sediment of wartime burdens and compromises, the unresolved tensions of nineteen-thirties pop culture. Eustache sees radical utopias and libertine dreams shattered by workaday troubles and intimate crises. His young Parisians' breezy erotic sophistication masks a streetwise urban populism that's as artistically fertile as it is politically risky; their range of intimate disasters has the feel and tone of epic clashes. (2016)

Both films are able to illustrate the changes which have occurred in wider society, while switching between depictions of that society and the stories of a few individuals. While Russell and Eustache are not the only filmmakers to have worked in this way, each film provides a magnificent example of a director narrowing and widening the focus of their story at will, while never losing sight of the overall point that's being made.

While we've examined the time in which *The Devils* was first released, and many consider the film's content to be ahead of its time (at least in terms of what could be shown on screen), it is perhaps worth considering the possibility that the film might not have been possible had Russell waited much longer. The political climate was changing in the UK, first signalled by Heath's election win in 1970 before being fully cemented with the 1979 victory of Margaret Thatcher (between these two Conservative prime ministers there was a half-decade of Labour rule, which ended so catastrophically it would see the party reduced to opposition for the next 18 years). Thatcher had little time for the arts, and set about slashing grants while barely tolerating artistic endeavours which looked as if they may turn a profit. The right wing of the party, which had begun to mutter under Heath, were now in full voice, and if budget cuts weren't problematic enough, the entertainment industry found itself under pressure to churn out bland, homogenous and, ideally, lucrative product:

> Enterprise in 1980s and early 1990s British culture largely refers to the massive privatization of previously public industries [....] Because Thatcherism had reworked several locations of traditional conservative value, ideal national image was couched in revivals of an older, aristocratic, and patrician tradition, particularly focused on the tastes, values, and triumphs of the Georgians and Victorians. (Flanagan, 2009: 217)

This statement makes a good job of explaining how the clock had been turned back. Additionally, had the film occurred under Thatcher's premiership it would have been subjected to the scrutiny of James Ferman, a future BBFC secretary who was widely viewed as a nightmare for those filmmakers who served up contentious fare.[7] Unlike John Trevelyan, the censor in charge when *The Devils* was classified for theatrical exhibition, Ferman did not cut an accommodating or progressive figure (at least not while in office). It is rather strange to think that the film may have been treated more fairly in earlier times when different political and cultural climates were in place. As such, the film's very existence may be the only thing that makes it a product of its time.

Madeleine visits the convent.

In his book *State of the Nation*, Michael Billington notes that the 1980s saw musicals become the dominant form on the UK stage, with the actors and technicians who had previously been the envy of the world being effectively sidelined (2007). The entrepreneurial aspect of musical theatre was very much in line with Thatcher's thinking, and media which came cap in hand was not particularly welcomed by the government of the day. In 1980, Thatcher's first full year as prime minister, UK film production was at its lowest point since the beginning of World War I. The subsequent abolition of the Eady Levy, a tax break scheme which had proven attractive to overseas companies looking to film in the UK, further hastened the decline. While there's an outside chance that *The Devils* could have been made under Thatcher (on a much reduced budget, and, post-Eady Levy, probably without American money), there is a high probability that it would have been distorted by a desire to attack the then-government and their draconian approach to the arts; although Thatcher was not quick to put her hand in her pocket when it came to financing creative works, her very tenure provided an abundance of fuel for cultural endeavours. The largely apolitical Russell's only political film may have redirected its attentions towards those considered responsible for the relative paucity of its budget, which in time would have relegated the film's status to that of a dated anti-Thatcher footnote. Despite the pressures Russell may have been under in 1971, his clarity of vision for *The Devils* went largely undisturbed; a decade later, the temptation to take a shot at those leading the country may well have been too great for a director not known for his restraint, and giving in to such impulses would have both diluted the film's message and shackled it to its time.

It's also worth considering where the film fits in with Russell's output up to the point of its release. There seems to be a fairly natural progression from a reasonably controversial (if relatively orthodox) literary adaptation (*Women in Love*, naked wrestling and all) to an overcooked composer biopic (*The Music Lovers*, with its infamously marketable axis of a marriage between a homosexual and a nymphomaniac) to something as brazenly left-field as *The Devils*. In terms of controversy, each of these films easily outdid their immediate predecessors—before *Women in Love* there was another, perfunctory book adaptation, *Billion Dollar Brain* (1967), which featured Françoise Dorléac's final film appearance and was easily the strangest of the Harry Saltzman-produced Harry Palmer spy films. If proof is needed that Russell himself viewed *The Devils* as some sort of apex, it's worth noting that he quickly followed the film with that most family-friendly of all his works—Twiggy vehicle *The Boy Friend* (1971), a gentle musical entirely free of graphic content.

In career terms, *The Devils*, which topped the domestic box office for a full eight weeks, was about as good as it got for Russell. While *Mahler* (1974) found a wide audience and its follow-up *Tommy* (1975) became Russell's biggest commercial success, the intensity of *The Devils'* release remains unmatched in Russell's filmography: the movie played in London's West End alongside the films the director had made immediately before and after it; a series of well-publicised censorship problems had unfolded prior to the release; and there were some very vocal supporters and detractors (there's no such thing as bad publicity, after all). It marked the point where he firmly cemented his status as a household name in the UK; even those who hadn't seen his work would be aware (and, most probably, wary) of his reputation as a purveyor of X-certificate hat-in-lap fare, and his name became a byword for the outré and controversial. In the year following the film's release, the *Monty Python* team would present a parodic TV sketch bearing Russell's name, long before the director himself would turn to self-parody.[8]

The Devils also saw Russell enter the realm of the auteur, with the presence of his name quickly diluting any of the performances, or indeed any of the action, featured in his subsequent films; to varying extents, this branding of sorts remained a selling point for the rest of his days. In the space of a couple of years, his situation had lurched from being a director who served his material to quite the opposite: at the time of its initial release, *Women in Love* was widely considered to be a D. H. Lawrence adaptation, while *The Devils*—despite also being based in part on a book by a highly revered author—was purely thought of as 'a Ken Russell movie' (and the opening titles mark it out as 'Ken Russell's film of *The Devils*', with the film's two celebrated authors of its source materials relegated to the hinterland of the end credits). The following chapter will attempt to separate out the authorial ingredients of the film.

FOOTNOTES

1. *Performance*'s producer Sandy Lieberson would go on to work with Ken Russell on *Mahler* and *Lisztomania*.
2. Stanley Kubrick asked that *A Clockwork Orange* be withdrawn from UK distribution in 1973, following a series of death threats made to his family in the wake of several serious crimes which were purportedly linked to the film. Warner Bros. granted this request but reintroduced the film to UK cinemas shortly after Kubrick's death in 1999 (the same year in which Warners' *The Exorcist* was finally granted a BBFC certificate for home viewing), and subsequently gave the film a UK video release.
3. Pathé News, a mainstay in cinemas for decades, only stopped being produced in 1970 when it could no longer compete with televised news.
4. Russell would voluntarily return to the framing device with *The Devils*' follow-up *The Boy Friend*, which saw Sandy Wilson's French-set musical of the same name staged by a struggling English theatre troupe. Many years later, Russell's *Salome's Last Dance* presented Oscar Wilde's 1891 work *Salome* as a play within the film.
5. *The Devils* featured a then-active Labour Member of Parliament who served under Wilson in the form of Andrew Faulds, who played Rangier. Glenda Jackson, another frequent Russell

collaborator (she'd won an Oscar for *Women in Love*) and the director's first choice for the role of Sister Jeanne, would also go on to become a Labour MP.

6. *Out 1* would also address the death of the 1960s, albeit in a culturally specific manner, given that the decade had effectively ended a couple of years early in France with the civil unrest of May 1968. Rivette would go on to make the epic two-part Joan of Arc film *Jeanne la pucelle* (1994), which culminated in a most unfair and horrific (but by no means graphic) burning at the stake as rattling as the one featured in *The Devils*.

7. Ferman was a much mellowed character as the years progressed, and he didn't seem to have any big problem with *The Devils*. He actually considered the US cut of the film to be a travesty, and in 1995 helped introduce a BBC showing of the original UK theatrical version.

8. The sketch, titled 'Ken Russell's Gardening Club (1958)', first aired in a 1972 episode of the third series of *Monty Python's Flying Circus*. The same series featured equally funny parodies of the work of two other controversial filmmakers: Sam Peckinpah ('Salad Days') and Pier Paolo Pasolini ('The Third Test Match'). Like Russell, the Pythons themselves were no strangers to material considered outré, and religious controversy would also catch up with them in due course with the release of their film *Life of Brian* (1979).

Chapter 2: Authorship and Adaptation

The Devils is often viewed, quite understandably, as being pure Ken Russell, but the influence of the two acknowledged sources on his screenplay should not be overlooked. A common view is that much of the historical information in the film was gleaned from Aldous Huxley's 1952 book *The Devils of Loudun*, and the dialogue was influenced by (or lifted from) John Whiting's 1961 play *The Devils*. The temporal nature of a film means it can be consumed with an economy that's in sharp contrast to the investment required to read a book, and movies can be widely, simultaneously distributed and accessed in a way which isn't practical for a stage play—which, as André Bazin astutely pointed out, 'reaches only a privileged cultural or monied minority' (1967: 53). On the basis of its consumability, Russell's film has become the overarching version of these events, and is the work which gave the story the most publicity and notoriety (Nakahara, 2004: 128). Both of the film's credited sources allow for interesting correlations with Russell's film, but what is often passed over is that Whiting's play was based on Huxley's book—therefore the film is based on both a book *and* a play that was based on that same book, meaning Russell adapts Huxley both directly and indirectly; with this in mind, a straightforward bifurcation of *The Devils*' screenplay isn't really possible. Whiting died within a couple of years of his play's premiere so did not live to see Russell's adaptation, but, perhaps not too surprisingly, some post-1971 productions of the play seem to have been heavily influenced by the film; this throws up valid questions regarding both adaptation and the film's status as the definitive, overruling take on these historical events.[1]

The Devils could easily be viewed as a film in which the literary works it's based on 'simply serve to supply the film-maker with characters and adventures largely independent of their literary framework', with these elements achieving an autonomy which largely renders 'the original works [...] no longer anything more than an accidental and almost superfluous manifestation' (Bazin, 1967: 53). However, any assessment that Russell has simply plucked the core action and characters from Huxley and Whiting and done exactly as he's pleased would not be a fair one; despite its profile being much higher than either of its credited sources, *The Devils* is very much a film which carefully, selectively draws from both the book and the play.

As it came first, Huxley's book is a natural starting point when it comes to delineating the sources of Russell's film. While there is a great deal of useful historical information in the book, it seems more likely that Russell was attracted to Huxley's style, spirit and methodology. Joseph Gomez notes how 'Huxley is not a biographer who meticulously subjects himself to the limitations of specific sources [....] Rather, he submerges himself in the history and culture of an age, [...] creat[ing] a controlling vision which shapes his work' (1976: 118). Such a description is very much in line with Russell's approach to *The Devils* and indeed his other biographical films from *The Debussy Film* on (see chapter 1). In terms of historical accuracy, Marc Bridle notes that 'Russell's film remains, at least in terms of fact, quite close to what Huxley recounts' (2004). *The Devils of Loudun* is an arcane documentary novel that's a far cry from the garden-variety biography, and the book's esoteric nature is amplified by its frequently untranslated passages (usually French, sometimes Latin), signalling that Huxley is writing for the few, not the many (this is in sharp contrast to Russell, who, as noted earlier, frequently went out of his way to be inclusive when dealing with lofty subject matter). In their respective takes on Grandier's story Huxley and Russell share a desire to make a serious point by capturing the essence, mood and spirit of the time and place, avoiding getting too weighed down by the minutiae of seventeenth-century life. As such, the tenor of both works is remarkably similar.

Barré (left) tortures Grandier.

Huxley's book begins with an air of mischief, and although the author's humour and sarcasm frequently shine through the work, it's not long before we're taken off on a tangent, away from Grandier's narrative, as Huxley grapples with some big philosophical fish as he examines the need for transcendence. It's incredibly dense stuff, and a weight is attached to these passages which seems to make the main Grandier/Loudun story breeze by in comparison. As one progresses through the book, it becomes clear that Huxley, while obviously fascinated by the events he's covering, is using them as frequent jumping-off points for discussions which relate what happened in Loudun to our times. Tribalism is covered in a way which explicitly links it to the twentieth century Huxley knew, and even the inclusive, progressive Grandier doesn't escape such treatment:

> Grandier's prime reason for disliking the monks was the fact that he himself was a secular priest and as loyal to his caste as the good soldier is loyal to his regiment, the good undergraduate to his school, the good Communist or Nazi to his party. Loyalty to organization A always entails some degree of suspicion, contempt or downright loathing of organizations, B, C, D and all the rest. (Huxley, 1952: 26)

Gomez makes the excellent point that Huxley's suspension of the narrative (and subsequent reduction of the dramatic impact) is precisely what allows us as readers to correlate Grandier's predicament with very modern concerns (1976: 122). Huxley was a quite brilliant writer, and his wide-ranging abilities mark him out as one of the greatest authors of the twentieth century, but it's the way in which he's structured *The Devils of Loudun* which makes it a particularly astonishing achievement. In carving out spaces in the book where the reader can breathe, absorb and reflect, he teleports Grandier's Loudun to the present day with quite chilling effect. While Russell's film provides little in the way of oases of calm amidst the *Sturm und Drang*, it does mirror the book's ability to send out warnings both for its time and the future. As Chuck Palahniuk put it: 'If you don't know what comes next, take a good long look at what came before' (2011). While the structure of Russell's film doesn't allow him the luxury of flashing forward to illustrate persecution in generally more enlightened times (Huxley can reference the behaviour of the likes of Hitler and Stalin much more readily and explicitly on the page), you'd do well to get through the movie and avoid connecting the despotic behaviour depicted with at least one other event which has occurred between the 1600s and now. As such, *The Devils* stands as a sort of *film à clef* for the ages, with the main players in the story finding numerous counterparts in the centuries which have elapsed since the death of Urbain Grandier.

The point made by Gomez above also reminds us how Russell, unlike Huxley, is chained to depicting events which occur in a specific, semi-enlightened time when reason and superstition lived happily side by side and the earth was simultaneously round and flat. Huxley observes this as:

> This temple of science, which is at the same time a magician's laboratory and a side show at a country fair, is a most expressive symbol of that strange agglomeration of incongruities, the seventeenth-century mind [....] The scientific spirit was already vigorously alive. But no less vigorously alive was the spirit of the medicine man and the witch. (1952: 45)

Quite where religion fits in between magic and science is probably a very subjective matter. As Gomez notes, Huxley also outlines how 'the beliefs of organized religion flourish today without any necessary beliefs in the supernatural' (1976: 122). From these quotes, we can perhaps deduce where Huxley feels religion as peddled by Richelieu et al. lies on the spectrum. However, it is cold comfort to think that the world has progressed to a stage where we now know better than to burn supposed heretics, yet still find other ways in which to demonise, persecute, ostracise and marginalise; Huxley makes it quite clear that we haven't evolved nearly as much as we think we have. While the milieu in Russell's film does not allow him to extend beyond Grandier's time, it nonetheless does contain a very specific, recognisable institution in the form of the Catholic Church, which connects the respective times of Grandier, Huxley, Whiting, Russell—and ourselves. That is not to say the Church hasn't changed or evolved in any way since the time in which Urbain Grandier was burned alive, but its very presence in both the film and present day proves that we can't simply dismiss all that's depicted as belonging to a distant, alien past—and that's before one considers any analogies or parallels.

As *The Devils of Loudun* comes to a close, Huxley provides a scintillating epilogue which is very much rooted in the present, and even in the final pages we're being asked some pretty big questions as the author tries to work out where both individuals and wider society should go from here:

> In order to escape from the horrors of insulated selfhood most men and women choose, most of the time, to go neither up nor down, but sideways. They identify

themselves with some cause wider than their own immediate interests, but not degradingly lower and, if higher, higher only within the range of current social values. (1952: 314)

From this, it's clear that Huxley sees the scope of his project as much broader than simply essaying the sorry fate of Urbain Grandier. The book sees the priest's story covered expertly and exhaustively, yet Huxley obviously had no intention of the work being limited to a simple historical document; *The Devils of Loudun* asks questions which span way beyond Grandier's predicament and time. In one of his letters, Huxley made it clear 'that philosophy is best expounded through a biography' (Smith, 1969, as cited in Gomez, 1976: 117). The biographical form of *The Devils of Loudun* allows the author to quickly fill up the book with factual content before it overspills into philosophical arguments which are of much greater concern (and interest) to Huxley than Grandier's life and death—which is perfectly understandable, as these questions affect us all and not just one man. Huxley goes on:

> How can we have the good without the evil, a high civilization without saturation bombing or the extermination of religious and political heretics? The answer is that we cannot have it so long as our self-transcendence remains merely horizontal. When we identify ourselves with an idea or a cause we are in fact worshiping something homemade, something partial and parochial, something that, however noble, is yet all too human. (1952: 314)

Huxley is arguing the need for man to break through the ceiling he's built for himself, and to venture somewhere beyond the well-trodden path of his own experience (in chapter 5 we'll take a slightly closer look at the self-transcendence he mentions, not for the only time, here). This illustrates what an ambitious, probing and sophisticated work *The Devils of Loudun* is, and even if Russell is largely unable to bring the more esoteric and philosophical nature of it to the screen, he did at least make a good fist of capturing the more linear narrative of the book, and embellished it with a message much in line with Huxley's sentiments.

Although Russell has oft been accused of playing very fast and loose with the facts when it comes to his version of the Loudun possessions, it seems that even Huxley was not beyond a bit of artistic license when it came to his interpretation of events:

> Undoubtedly, *The Devils of Loudun* owed something of its réclame to its 'interdisciplinary' construction. It is a history book that can't be bothered with dates. It is a work of completely undocumented sociology, backed up by Huxley's credit alone. It is a non-fiction novel that also expounds metaphysical philosophies. If I neglect to mention demonic possession, that's only because the author doesn't believe that it actually occurred. (Keefe, 2005)

The book, it should be said, does contain a bibliography, but the comment above does highlight the desire of Huxley, just like Russell many years later, to get to the heart of the matter without becoming bogged down by apparently needless historical detail.

Russell's shiny Loudun, as designed by Derek Jarman, makes a very bold statement, with the city's gleaming, precise masonry the antithesis of the crumbling, decaying stonework which may have been expected in any 'realistic' depiction of the period. Tony Peake notes that 'what Russell wanted from the design was sufficient freshness to bring home the excesses of seventeenth-century Loudun to a contemporary audience', and mentions how Russell and Jarman looked to the architecture of Fritz Lang's *Metropolis* (1927) for inspiration (2011). While the Loudun of the film would not meet with present-day health and hygiene standards, the city does seem remarkably clean considering both the era and its ravaging by plague. The Russell–Jarman vision of Loudun is a visually striking one, and from our first glimpse of Grandier delivering a stentorian speech against a backdrop of stark, white brickwork (do those pillars that flank him loosely mirror the hoods worn in the court which later convicts the priest?), it's clear that this is a very different world than the viewer might reasonably have expected, yet is a more relatable environment for contemporary audiences than wall-to-wall mud and squalor. The relatively sophisticated appearance of Loudun further contrasts with the medieval treatment meted out to Grandier, which would be slightly easier to accept were it to happen in, say, the renaissance-suppressing milieu of *Hard to Be a God* (2013), in which intellectuals are routinely executed in a world wilfully stuck in the middle ages. The film's representation of the city is also very much at odds with Huxley's description of Loudun as hosting 'the usual dirty streets, the customary gamut of smells, from wood smoke to excrement, from geese to incense, from baking bread to horses, swine and unwashed humanity' (1952: 11–12).

Grandier addresses the people of Loudun at Sainte-Marthe's funeral.

Frequently in literary adaptations, the depiction of a place (or person) on screen is often quite jarring to those with a mental image created by the source material, and just as the physical appearance of Loudun may be sufficiently surprising to those who've come to the film via Huxley's book, there are other changes and omissions of note. The film's Urbain Grandier, as played by Oliver Reed in the best of his screen performances, is a good approximation of the hubristic character Huxley painted for us. However, there are a couple of notable characters whose relationships with Grandier are shown in a very unbalanced way in the film. Trincant, for one, is described by Huxley as being 'the parson's best friend, his staunchest and most resolute ally against the monks, the *Lieutenant Criminel* and the rest of his adversaries' (1952: 34). In the film, this isn't established, which greatly reduces the impact of Grandier's betrayal of his friend in sleeping with Phillipe, Trincant's daughter, when he's supposed to be tutoring her in Latin. Huxley pointedly notes that 'to abuse such trust would be the blackest of crimes. And yet its very blackness was a reason for committing it' (1952: 35). The film sees Trincant and Grandier's relationship fast-tracked to the point where they're involved in a physical fight over Phillipe's pregnancy; Grandier, in what is possibly the film's most absurd moment, defends himself against Trincant's rapier by using a stuffed crocodile that he'd recently, conveniently thrown out of the window of the house of Madeleine's mother. As Grandier mocks and laughs at Trincant, his parting words and riposte to the magistrate's furious 'I'll see you in Hell!' are 'Walking on a living pavement of aborted bastards, no doubt'—an abrasive rewording of Huxley's more refined 'in Hell the damned walk on a living pavement, tessellated with the tiny carcasses of unbaptized babies' (1952: 33). This highly unpleasant reply shows an ugly, self-serving side to the priest that's virtually indefensible; even Grandier's most ardent supporter would be unlikely to contest that these words are borne of Malthusian concern. The line, as spoken in the film, is but one instance of Russell adeptly taking non-dialogue from Huxley's prose and putting it into the mouths of his characters—other good examples are Sister Jeanne condescendingly telling Madeleine that she has 'the face of a virgin martyr in a picture book' and Laubardemont proclaiming that 'today's loyalty is no guarantee against tomorrow's rebellion' (Huxley, 1952: 105, 61).

The gravely offended Trincant, in Russell as in Huxley, goes on to become a highly influential foe as Grandier's downfall is mapped out, but in the film there is no real hint of the friendship and trust which existed between the two men prior to the Phillipe incident. The film also misses a trick in not making it clear that the lead judge in the court which convicts Grandier is actually Trincant; while the official's face is concealed beneath a sinister white hood, the voice clearly belongs to actor John Woodvine. If this was more obvious, it would underline how the magistrate has avenged his family, but as it stands the Trincant of the film is an infuriatingly compromised character who sees his potentially very rich arc in the story truncated at both ends. While Trincant is robbed of some big moments (being bitterly betrayed, taking sweet revenge), it says much that the character nonetheless makes a lasting impression via what may be, in Woodvine, the film's least showy performer. Trincant may largely refrain from indulging in the histrionics favoured by likes of Barré, Louis and Mignon, but Woodvine's interpretation—coupled with the rounded character served up by Huxley—leaves one wanting much more from the magistrate than Russell is prepared to give.

Baron de Laubardemont is another character in the film whose relationship with Grandier is only shown after it has soured, and the film sees the two men at loggerheads from their very first meeting. Huxley portrays their friendship as being as one-sided as the one between Grandier and Trincant, with the priest this time being on the business end of duplicity. Huxley draws Laubardemont as the most reptilian character in his story:

The scorned Phillipe.

> His career was a demonstration of the fact that, in certain circumstances, crawling is a more effective means of locomotion than walking upright, and that the best crawlers are also the deadliest biters. All his life Laubardemont had systematically crawled before the powerful and bitten the defenceless. (1952: 64)

Again, with the luxury of a good three centuries of the arts following the death of Grandier, Huxley cataphorically cites a much more relatable reference point for his readers when describing Laubardemont:

> In appearance and manner the Baron had modeled himself, two hundred and some odd years before the event, on Dickens's Uriah Heep. The long, squirming body, the damp hands incessantly rubbed, the constant protestations of humility and good will—all were there. And so was the underlying malignancy, so was the ruthless eye to the main chance. (ibid.)

We get virtually nothing of this Laubardemont in the film—the only time the Baron ostensibly shows respect to Grandier is when he, *sans* written edict, first arrives in Loudun and declares his unwieldy title ('Baron de Laubardemont, First President of the Court of Appeal, Member of the Council for the State and now His Majesty's Special Commissioner for the demolition of the fortifications of Loudun, at your service, Father'). While we must remember that Russell, working within a very different structure from Huxley, needed to cut, conflate and shift around his material for the sake of expedience, there is something disappointing about only seeing Laubardemont as openly hostile to Grandier. In Huxley's book, the scheming Baron offers his friendship to Grandier even as the priest's enemies are mobilising, and is shown to have:

> [I]nvited Grandier and his friends to a farewell dinner, at which he drank the parson's health, assured him of undying friendship and promised to do everything in his power to assist him in his struggle against a cabal of unscrupulous enemies. So much kindness, and offered so generously, so spontaneously! Grandier was moved almost to tears. (1952: 145)

Baron de Laubardemont rides into town.

This illustrates how convincing an actor Laubardemont really was, as the worldly, wily and cynical Grandier was generally not one to be hoodwinked by anyone. It is a pity that the film does not show us this side of the Baron, but what Russell does with the character is still pretty special. The late Dudley Sutton, as Laubardemont, is the only performer to significantly encroach on the limelight which is almost exclusively commanded by Reed and Vanessa Redgrave (who plays Jeanne). Laubardemont, in the film, makes for a perfectly hissable antagonist, but he could perhaps have become one of the great screen villains had Russell included the other side of the man as described by Huxley. Laubardemont survives the film, and leaves the story with a swagger akin to that of the Grandier seen in the film's early stages. In the book, however, Huxley barely contains his glee as he notes the Baron's end and the ignominious fates of his issue:

> At about the same time [the end of the Thirty Years' War], obscure and out of favour, Laubardemont died. His only son had turned highwayman and been killed. His last

surviving daughter had been obliged to take the veil and was now an Ursuline at Loudun, under her father's old protégée. (1952: 270)

While the characterisations of Laubardemont and Trincant in the film suffer more through omission than anything else, confusion arises (at least for scholars of the book) in the film when characters are given lines which belong to others in Huxley's story, which understandably alters the disposition of the given character. This is especially obvious when the Philippe of Huxley sees her words snatched from her by Russell:

> Confession succeeded confession. The parson listened attentively [....] And then the day came when she made her slip of the tongue, when, instead of 'him,' she said 'you,' and then tried to withdraw the word, became confused and, under his questioning, burst into tears and confessed the truth. (Huxley, 1952: 39)

Huxley's Philippe cuts a far more sympathetic figure than the one seen in Russell's film, in which she petulantly acts out when confessing to Grandier (as a side note, both Whiting and Russell go with the spelling 'Phillipe', whereas in Huxley 'Philippe' is preferred—hence this book's seemingly inconsistent spelling of the name). In Huxley, there's an innocence to this young woman who develops what is little more than a schoolgirl crush on her Latin teacher, yet in the film she crashes into the action as a brattish, spiteful and very annoying female who's clearly getting in Grandier's way once he's had his fun. The verbal slip-up (she's referring to the man she loves in the third person, before lapsing into the second) as quoted above—which signals a shy, inexperienced, unconfident girl—is given to Russell's Madeleine, who goes on to enjoy a tender, loving relationship with Grandier which develops into marriage; this is poles apart from the sordid affair he had with Phillipe, which culminated in an unwanted pregnancy. Thus, the best of Huxley's Philippe is transferred to Madeleine in the film, and we're left with a most unsympathetic character who, abandoned and with a baby, delights in watching Grandier's execution. When we get to Whiting's play, we'll see yet another complication concerning the roles of Phillipe and Madeleine.

The contrast between Russell and Huxley's depictions of Madeleine and Phillipe/Philippe is obvious in the way in which both characters exit the two stories: the Madeleine of the book ends up meekly sloping off to a convent, whereas in the film she's afforded slightly more dignity as she's seen walking away from the rubble of Loudun, destination unknown. The fate of Philippe in the book is recorded by Huxley in a way which both elicits sympathy for the young woman and underlines the shame which the whole sorry saga has brought on her previously esteemed father and family:

> Under quiet but persistent pressure Trincant resigned. Instead of selling […] his post, he gave it away to Louis Moussaut—but gave it on a condition. The young lawyer would not become Loudun's Public Prosecutor until after his marriage with Philippe Trincant. For Henri IV, Paris had been worth a Mass. For M. Moussaut a good job was worth his fiancée's lost virginity and the ribaldry of the Protestants. After a quiet wedding, Philippe settled down to serve her sentence—forty years of loveless marriage. (1952: 62–63)

This highlights a very different character from the jeering, bloodthirsty woman who cheerfully takes in the sight of Grandier's death, viewing the infernal proceedings from a vantage point that Huxley, describing the spots taken up by ghoulish tourists, brilliantly terms a 'stake-side seat' (1952: 195). Huxley's Philippe is a naïve young woman, taken in and subsequently jettisoned by someone she both trusted and looked up to, and is to be pitied. Going by this portrayal, Urbain Grandier deserves at least some of the brickbats which are hurled his way—but Russell doesn't want to draw audience sympathies away from Grandier, therefore his Phillipe is demonised as someone who's brought her predicament upon herself, and is to be loathed for the *schadenfreude* she experiences as she watches the author of her misfortune burn at the stake.

Grandier stands before the court.

Huxley's book is an incredibly detailed account, so bringing it to the screen (and stage) required some judicious thinning out of the material. That said, there are at least two characters from the book who do not appear in the film yet could reasonably have been expected to figure. The first is Jean d'Armagnac, Governor of Loudun and friend of Grandier. As the film begins, Georges de Sainte-Marthe is said to be the city's recently-deceased Governor, with temporary emergency powers transferred to Grandier; the real-life equivalent for this is found in prominent man of letters Scévole de Sainte-Marthe, whose death led to his coveted place among Loudun's intellectual elite being taken by Grandier (Bourne, n.d.). It's quite a stretch to get from that to the transfer of administrative power which occurs in the film, and with such deviations from recorded history one would not be overly surprised to see Gilles de Rais and Marie Antoinette wander into the action.

D'Armagnac would certainly have been a useful character to bring in to the film; as the film stands there is a distinct lack of friends in high places for Grandier, which may make him rather more heroic in his plight but equally serves to make his lofty status less credible. Had the other side of Laubardemont, as discussed earlier, been shown in the film then d'Armagnac would have been of further interest as another victim of that smiling assassin. Just as with the dinner he throws for Grandier, the duplicitous Laubardemont turns up to the baptism of one of d'Armagnac's children, which the Governor views as a touching sign of real friendship—'but the Baron had no friends and was devoted only to the powerful. D'Armagnac wielded no effective power; he was merely the favourite of a King who had invariably shown himself too weak to say no to his first minister [Richelieu]' (Huxley, 1952: 64). The lack of respect afforded to d'Armagnac is shared by Cardinal Richelieu, who Huxley describes as viewing the Governor as 'merely an unimportant little courtier', with such disdain extended to Loudun as being 'a nest of potentially dangerous Huguenots' (1952: 61). Russell was obviously wary of cluttering his film with too many major characters and introducing an overly complicated political narrative thread, but d'Armagnac's presence would have been welcomed as it would have allowed for scenes in which Grandier could discuss his woes with a high-up ally; as it is, Grandier is effectively an island in a sea of injustice.

Also notable by his absence in the film is François Leclerc du Tremblay, better known as Father Joseph. The original *éminence grise* was known as Cardinal Richelieu's right-hand man and seems ripe for a film which is very much concerned with skulduggery within the Church. Father Joseph does feature in *The Devils of Loudun*, and prior to that book Huxley had actually devoted an entire work, *Grey Eminence* (1941), to the influential Capuchin friar. Some may feel that the very nature of an *éminence grise* dictates that they are largely unseen, or at least not seen to do the work they carry out, but *The Devils* is a film that's quite happy to lay bare what goes on behind the scenes of the Church. *Grey Eminence* includes a potted history of the events at Loudun, in which Father Joseph's connection to the case is noted:

> Such was the friar's reputation that people now connected his name with every strange and questionable occurrence of the time. Thus, not only had he planned the killing of Gustavus Adolphus; he was also deeply implicated in that *cause célèbre* [...] — the case of Father Urbain Grandier of Loudun and the nuns he was said to have bewitched. (Huxley, 1941: 207)

Father Joseph's involvement, at least on a superficial level, in the circus that was the Loudun possessions would not have been difficult to work into Russell's film, and we can only speculate as to why such an important figure does not make the cut. Again, Russell's need to streamline his story perhaps meant that there was only room for Richelieu, the *éminence rouge*, and Father Joseph's presence, even if permitted by the film's duration, may have caused confusion among audiences. Perhaps, like Huxley, Russell felt that Joseph belonged in his own separate work, although the film could have carried a brief appearance by the character in the same way that *Grey Eminence* references Loudun. Richelieu does not come out of *The Devils* well, and along with Laubardemont and Barré is one of the true villains of the piece. Interestingly, Huxley somewhat absolves both shades of *éminence*:

> In the Loudun affair, neither Richelieu nor Father Joseph exhibited anything worse than weakness. Thinking to win a little popularity by getting himself associated with a case that had aroused [...] fanatical enthusiasm, Richelieu gave money to the exorcists, who had been summoned in 1633 to work upon the nuns. It was a regrettable move, which seemed to lend a certain official sanction to the proceedings. As for Father Joseph's intervention, this consisted in a visit paid to Loudun [...] and a hasty retreat to Paris. Loudun was a hornets' nest; the case was suffered to take its

horrible course. On the 18th of August 1634, Grandier was duly burned alive. (1941: 208)

It is notable that Huxley here presents the snowballing events (and the endgame) of Loudun as something which has taken on a feral nature which may even have gone beyond the control of both Richelieu and Joseph, with the latter clearly finding the situation far too hot to handle. Conversely, Russell's Richelieu rules with a rod of iron and the events at Loudun are shown as being completely under the influence of the Cardinal, barring the formalities of getting the king to renege on the promise he made to Sainte-Marthe—Huxley states that the real Governor, d'Armagnac, 'had received private assurances from the King [...] that, even if the rest of the castle were destroyed, the donjon would be left standing' (1952: 61). While the Richelieu of the film appears to be completely intransigent, in *The Devils of Loudun* he's said to seesaw between taking the supernatural seriously and dismissing it outright (Huxley, 1952: 142).

Before we leave *The Devils of Loudun* and focus on Whiting's play, there's a nagging detail in Russell's film which tends to confound anyone who cares to question it: after Jeanne has been subjected to the highly degrading exorcism, a smiling Trincant announces that 'the Devil, it seems, departed from the Mother Superior at 10:45 precisely', and the pocket watch he extends to confirm this is spat upon by a scowling Phillipe (yet another charming moment from this version of her). Trincant's words make little sense, as they refer to something that was cut out of the film at the request of the censor: the result of Jeanne's bowel movement following her roughly administered holy water clyster. Without this incident, Trincant's comment sounds like a random phrase, or a punchline detached from its preceding narrative, and is something which really should have been fixed prior to release. Huxley is able to deftly bridge this gap for us:

> M. Adam came, bringing with him [...] the huge brass syringe of Molièresque farce and seventeenth-century medical reality. A quart of holy water was ready for him. The syringe was filled, and M. Adam approached the bed on which the Mother Superior was lying. Perceiving that his last hour was at hand, Asmodeus threw a fit. In vain. The Prioress's limbs were pinioned [...] and, with the skill born of long practice, M. Adam administered the miraculous enema. Two minutes later, Asmodeus had taken his departure. (1952: 113)

If you really care to do so, you can briefly glimpse the quite unholy mess on the altar as the camera fleetingly tracks along in the shot immediately following Phillipe's spitting. Huxley's description of this grim procedure is a great example of the way in which he adroitly balances humour and horror, a skill that Russell also displays in his film. The reference to Molière is yet another instance of Huxley using a more recognisable name in order to pull the reader into the action (or drag the events into the present); while Molière was indeed around during Grandier's lifetime, he was just a boy when the priest was executed and had yet to embark on his career as a playwright, but his name and work have endured in the centuries since *Tartuffe*, like Grandier, raised the hackles of the Catholic Church.

From left: Mignon, Laubardemont, Barré and Trincant hear Jeanne's claims.

Huxley's book, as has already been established, is a complex, labyrinthine affair which packs a great deal into a deceptively slim volume. It is not the sort of book which readily lends itself to adaptation of any kind, so when Peter Hall commissioned John Whiting to write a play for the Royal Shakespeare Company which would be based on *The Devils of Loudun*, we can only imagine the logistical nightmare Whiting experienced when faced with this imposing combination of bloody biography and deep philosophy. Whiting was a respected drama critic who himself made frequent forays into writing plays; both *Saint's Day* (1951) and *Marching Song* (1953) had marked him out as a capable and inventive playwright, although it wasn't until *The Devils* that he was considered to be breaking through as one of the best dramatists working in the UK. Unfortunately, testicular cancer claimed Whiting at the age of 45 (his death came just five months before that of Aldous

Huxley, who died from laryngeal cancer), but we can extrapolate from his body of work that he would have stayed fairly near the top of the UK theatre scene for many years. When looking at the film—which of course came after both Huxley and Whiting had told Grandier's story—it's useful to keep in mind how each retelling of the tale comes with a distinct authorial stamp:

> What the historian is faced with in *The Devils* is a story that has undergone considerable reinterpretation over the years. In the true style of overcooked historiography it has passed from mouth to mouth and received the mark of each interpreter's agenda on the way. (Bourne, n.d.)

Knowing where to start when adapting the book for the stage must have been quite the task, but it's clear that Whiting opted to strip away Huxley's philosophical musings and present the more stage-ready Grandier narrative. Soon into the play we encounter a character unfamiliar from the book in the form of the anachronistic Sewerman, who is as much a structural device as he is a full-blown character. The Sewerman pops up frequently to interact with Grandier and bring some lightheartedness to proceedings, although their encounters are not entirely without pathos, particularly in the play's latter stages. The main function of the character seems to be to prevent Grandier from breaking the fourth wall, and the points at which the Sewerman appears mark him out as a type of Greek chorus. The Sewerman not only performs an important technical role in the staging of the play but was no doubt a big help to Whiting as he was writing the piece—once he'd hit upon the idea of the Sewerman, a spine was in place which would allow the playwright to organise Grandier's story in a cohesive, theatrically viable manner (this is perhaps comparable to Huxley arranging Grandier's story in a way which would allow for the author's philosophical musings to be included). The Sewerman and Grandier do form something of a double act in the play, which, as in Huxley's book, highlights the priest's need for a foil which goes unmet in the film. As the final act draws to a close and the character he's spent virtually all of his time with is killed, the Sewerman briefly finds another to interact with in the form of Sister Jeanne:

Jeanne: What are they doing?

Sewerman: It's bits of the body they're after.

Jeanne: As relics?

> Sewerman: Don't try to comfort yourself. No, they want them as charms. There's a difference, you know (*he snatches a charred bone from one of the men*). They don't want to adore this. They want it to cure their constipation or their headache, to have it bring back their virility or their wife. They want it for love or hate (*he holds out the bone*). Do you want it for anything?
>
> *Jeanne shakes her head. The crowd has gone, the Sewerman goes. Jeanne is alone. She cries out in her own voice:*
>
> Jeanne: Grandier! Grandier! (Whiting, 1961: 114)

This is how the play ends, and the Sewerman, who's provided us with some fine (and much needed) levity over the course of the piece, is involved in a poignant moment as he offers a charred piece of the man he'd befriended to a woman who was instrumental in the death of that friend. The Sewerman's explanation as to why the crowds are coveting Grandier's remains alludes to Huxley's observation that, even in supposedly enlightened times, superstition was always ready to surface whenever the opportunity arose. In Whiting's play it's actually more affecting to see Jeanne refuse the bone she's offered at the end, whereas in Russell's film she doesn't have a choice in the matter as Laubardemont lobs a suitably phallic femur in her direction; at first, she recoils, before later using it as a sex aid. This is the only way she and Grandier will ever be together, and it's a desperate act, but by this stage Russell's demented Jeanne appears to not know if it's Pentecost or Assumption—Whiting's Jeanne, on the other hand, is a broken woman who is well aware of her part in this terrible chain of events. The Jeanne of the play cuts a more innocent figure than the one in the film, and Whiting illustrates this most effectively via a scene in which she prays for the mother, father and dog she left behind when she joined the convent.

One of the most obviously comic aspects of the film is the partnership of the chemist Adam and the surgeon Ibert (the latter renamed, as in both Huxley and Whiting this character is known as Mannoury). Ibert and Adam appear to be a hapless, conniving and sycophantic pair who are berated by Grandier when he catches them sadistically administering a selection of ineffective yet painful treatments to Madeleine de Brou's dying mother. In the film Adam (Brian Murphy, before the sitcom fame that's now

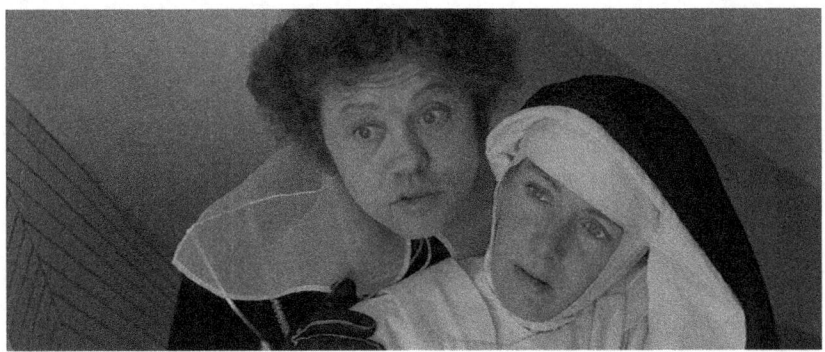

Laubardemont pays one last visit to Jeanne.

impossible for UK viewers to disassociate him from) and Ibert (Russell regular Max Adrian, who played Father Barré in the first stage production) frequently threaten to take the film permanently into *Monty Python* territory (they could quite easily turn up in *Monty Python and the Holy Grail* [1975]), which makes their hand in Grandier's fate all the more disturbing.[2] Grandier dismisses them as buffoons, but it is they who observe his secret marriage and can't wait to spill the beans, wildly embellishing as they pour out the details to Laubardemont et al. They're seen in court as Grandier is sentenced to death, and the expression on Ibert's face at the mention of a commemorative plaque that will be paid for by Grandier's estate is by far the most chilling moment involving this motley pair. The two gleefully take part in the shaving, humiliation and torture of Grandier, relishing dishing out even more savage treatment than that afforded to Mme de Brou. Huxley records the arrogance which eventually backfires on Grandier:

> They [Adam and Mannoury] invited sarcasm, they solicited the shafts of derision. With the merciless ferocity of a clever man who will go to any lengths for the sake of a laugh, the parson gave them what they asked for. In a very little while he had two new enemies. (1952: 31)

Whiting picks up the notion of the 'clever' priest, supplying Mannoury with an epithet he can level at Grandier while highlighting the resentment he and his partner feel towards the clergyman, which is based on Grandier's mockery of them as well as his social and sexual prowess:

Mannoury: You fell into his trap, Adam. Never engage Mister Clever.

Adam: He smelled of the widow woman. Filth.

Mannoury: Of course. He's just come from her.

Adam: After tickling himself in the confessional with the sins of young girls this morning—

Mannoury: He consummates himself in the widow's bed this afternoon—

Adam: And then comes and yawns in our faces.

Mannoury: Tonight—

Adam: Tonight he'll spend in some great house. D'Armagnac's, De Cerisay's. Fed, comforted, and flattered by the laughter of women. (1961: 17)

Although seething with envy, Mannoury and Adam still come across as two incorrigible gossips, an aspect of their characters that Whiting conveyed without furnishing them with the same amount of humour invested in the Sewerman. Russell takes these characterisations and grafts on a layer of absurdity which, in the play, isn't so much missing as dormant. As already mentioned, the horror is all the more unsettling when these two leering clowns eventually bare their teeth, and Russell's take on the chemist and the surgeon is one which crystallises Grandier's nightmare: it *would* be funny if it wasn't so terrifying.

Ibert (left) and Adam grovel and scheme.

If we're in any doubt as to the extent of the malice which lies in this seemingly bumbling pair, Russell explicitly conveys the delight in which Ibert, while watching Grandier die, speaks of the unfolding events to Phillipe's baby: 'Watch, bastard. See how your mother's honour was avenged. Lucky little bastard. It's not every day baby sees Daddy burned to death'. Phillipe revels in the moment of Grandier's death just as much as the chemist and the surgeon, and is seen cavorting with the pair as the priest meets his end at the stake—her previous petulance now transformed into full-bore cruelty.

In contrast, Whiting's Phillipe is markedly different from both the Huxley and Russell versions of the character, with the biggest and most obvious change being that the Phillipe in the play is a composite of Philippe and Madeleine. In both book and film, Grandier impregnates Philippe/Phillipe and then marries Madeleine, but the play sees Phillipe on the receiving end of both dubious honours. As such, and as is perhaps to be expected, this hybrid is a far more rounded character than either Russell's Madeleine or Phillipe, and the dichotomy that we're presented with in the film is notably absent in the play (although there is a very minor character in the form of the widow Ninon, who Grandier visits for purely carnal reasons, and who also appears in the book). When witnessing Russell's take on the two characters, the differences are so extreme that, beyond each being female and in a relationship with Grandier, it is hard to find much else to link them. Whiting's idea to combine the two characters seems borne as much from expedience as anything else, but his need to streamline did result in a more authentic characterisation. It is rather a pity that, after Whiting's sterling work, Russell separated the characters, which achieves little else other than bringing the parts into line with Huxley—and only on a very superficial level.

Phillipe's final scene in the play differs from her already contrasting departures in the book and the film, and in Whiting's version we have what is perhaps the most desolate of all three of her exits; described as 'monstrously pregnant', Phillipe is last seen to be leading an old man by the hand, referring to him as 'dear husband', and promising both a night of sexual adventure and a lifetime of marital bliss (1961: 112–113). This is possibly the bleakest ending for any of the incarnations of the character, as while the Philippe in Huxley plays out her days in a loveless marriage and the one in the film appears content to be horrible, Whiting presents us with a woman who has lost her great love (and possibly her mind) and is clutching at straws in the most undignified of manners.

Certainly, from an audience point of view, Whiting's Phillipe is the most sympathetic, and her final moments on the stage make for a sad, sorry sight.

Phillipe, as seen in the play, also neatly provides a way in which the relationship between Grandier and her father is established; a conversation between these three characters underlines the great respect Trincant has for Grandier (while highlighting the priest's imperious manner) and marks the beginning of Grandier and Phillipe's association:

Grandier: Do you speak any Latin?

Phillipe: A little.

Grandier: That's not enough.

Trincant: Unless—

Grandier: It's an exact language. Makes it possible to say just what you mean. That's rare nowadays. Don't you agree?

Phillipe: Yes, it is.

Trincant: Unless you, Father Grandier, would undertake the instruction.

Grandier: Of your daughter?

Trincant: Yes.

Grandier: I'm a busy man.

Trincant: Just one day a week. A few hours in the appreciation of finer things. It could be done by conversation. Perhaps the reading of suitable Latin verse.

Grandier: Very well.

Trincant: Shall we say Tuesday?

Grandier: No. Not Tuesday. (Whiting, 1961: 23)

In retaining d'Armagnac from the book, a character Russell would dispense with, Whiting is also able to further highlight how Grandier associated with the most high-ranking of officials of Loudun; Trincant was already a prominent figure in the city, and one considered inferior by Grandier, but a tête-à-tête with the governor is a sign of the high status the priest enjoys:

D'Armagnac: You don't make it easy for your friends, Grandier. Trincant has told me about his daughter. You have your whores. Why did you have to do this?

Grandier: It seemed a way.

D'Armagnac: A way to what?

Grandier: All worldly things have a single purpose for a man of my kind. Politics, power, the senses, riches, pride and authority. I choose them with the same care that you, sir, select a weapon. (1961: 65)

In the film this conversation occurs, more or less verbatim, between Fathers Grandier and Mignon, with the 'weapon' comment referring to Trincant. Although this is one of many examples of Russell using Whiting's dialogue, the impact of the scene in the film is diminished as we know that, despite sharing a title, Mignon and Grandier are not on equal footing (Grandier's status as *primus inter pares* is evidenced at Sainte-Marthe's funeral, where a ruffle of the hair is enough to entice the altar boys to abandon carrying the train of Mignon's robes in favour of Grandier's).

Father Mignon presents himself to a highly disappointed Jeanne.

While the above dialogue is by no means the only example of Russell transplanting Whiting's lines into the film, perhaps the biggest contribution Whiting made, as far as the film is concerned, was to process Huxley's book—as brilliant as the book is, it is a difficult work which provides few clues as to how it might be adapted. Whiting managed to take the book and extract a linear, focused narrative from it that played, on the stage, as a highly cohesive and, more pertinently, accessible piece of drama. Reading through the play, a lack of staginess is apparent and Whiting does write in what might be described as a very cinematic style (Gomez, 1976: 127). Any film based on a play faces common pitfalls (betrayal of the source medium, failure to exploit the possibilities of cinema), but Russell's movie is unlikely to be pegged as an adaptation of a theatrical piece by anyone unaware of the fact; ironically, John Whiting deserves at least some of the credit for this. While Russell did indeed add to and alter Whiting's work, the play performs the important task of turning some of Huxley's book into a performance piece, and one that's largely screen-ready. The play is the catalyst in the sequence of getting the story from the pages of the book to the cinema screen. Without Whiting's work on the logistics of the story and his refashioning of Huxley's material, the book would almost certainly have joined that group of allegedly 'unfilmable' classics.

Curiously, for all its appropriation of the play, the film passes up a fantastic speech by Laubardemont which seems perfectly suited to both Russell's version of the character and Dudley Sutton's performance:

> You are alive, and you know it. But when you are stretched out in that little room, with the pain screaming through you like a voice, let me tell you what you will think. First: how can man do this to man? Then: how can God allow it? Then: there can be no God. Then: there is no God. The voice of pain will grow stronger, and your resolution weaker. (Whiting, 1961: 101)

If Huxley's 'public lavatory' phrase (see chapter 4) is the most memorable line of his book and greatly inspired Russell's approach to the film, it seems reasonable to assume that the director also drew from the standout line in Whiting's play (which, ironically, isn't a piece of dialogue, but is just a stage direction), in which Grandier, post-torture, is described as 'a ridiculous, hairless, shattered doll' (1961: 110). This brilliant description is a most accurate one as we witness Oliver Reed's Grandier as he crawls (and is kicked) along the ground on his hellish journey to the stake.

In the same year that Whiting's play premiered, Jerzy Kawalerowicz's film *Mother Joan of the Angels* (*Matka Joanna od Aniołów*, 1961) won the Jury Prize at Cannes. This Polish film, although rather more loosely based on the same chain of events drawn on by Huxley,

Urged by the crowd, Mignon administers the kiss of peace to Grandier.

Whiting and Russell, concentrates on the lives of the nuns *after* Grandier has been burned at the stake. It's interesting for several reasons, one being that it plays as a sort of sequel to Russell's film (which, of course, was made a full decade later). As its UK PG rating signifies, *Mother Joan* is a film which lacks any particularly explicit depictions in what is a very sensational story, but it is nonetheless a haunting and troubling work which culminates in the destruction of another priest by the title character.

Kawalerowicz's film is worth considering, even if it didn't provide any source material for Russell—although the director did see *Mother Joan* roughly midway between its release and commencing work on *The Devils* (Phillips, 1970). If anything, *The Devils* is actually rather more likely to have been influenced by Czech film *Witchhammer* (*Kladivo na čarodějnice*, 1970), another movie based on a novel inspired by real-life 17th century witch trials. *Mother Joan of the Angels* picks up the story of Father Jean-Joseph Surin, a key figure in Huxley's book yet one who doesn't feature at all in the works of Whiting and Russell; there's a good reason for this—he didn't come to Loudun until after Grandier's time, but Huxley didn't have quite the same aim as playwright or filmmaker, both of whom clearly saw Grandier's death as the literally blazing climax of their respective works. Father Surin's story takes over the last quarter of Huxley's book once Grandier has been torched, and his importance to *The Devils of Loudun* is signalled in his prominent billing at the beginning of the bibliography, where the author refers to his work as a 'history of Grandier, Surin, Sœur Jeanne and the devils' (1952: 315). Surin is a completely different character from Grandier, and Huxley makes him sound more like Russell's Mignon, describing him as 'one of those frail, nervous beings in whom the sexual impulse is powerful almost to frenzy' (1952: 71).

The neurotic Surin of *Mother Joan*, who has travelled to Loudun to deal with the seemingly still-possessed nuns, becomes deeply involved with Joan/Jeanne to the point where he willingly takes on her demons and performs a double murder to ensure the evil spirits stay with him. In his novel *The Exorcist*—which contains a final outcome not entirely dissimilar to that of *Mother Joan*—William Peter Blatty merely notes that Surin went completely out of his mind following his encounter at Loudun (2011: 242). While the film of *Mother Joan* ultimately goes way over the top, the real Surin was certainly bowled over by the smoke and mirrors routine of Jeanne and company, writing in his catchily-titled *Science expérimentale des choses de l'autre vie acquise en la possession des Ursulines de Loudun* of 'the extraordinary things that I saw in the possessed persons', and the encounter completely ruined his life (1993). Predating the wild embellishment Russell would bring to the Loudun story—and going well beyond the much less sensational accounts provided by both Surin and Blatty—the climax of Kawalerowicz's film swims in melodrama that's at odds with its established severe formalism; the sensational ending feels almost tacked on, à la Blatty's own *The Exorcist III* (1990). While *Mother Joan of the Angels* does have an incongruously lurid fate in store for the priest, it does operate in a sphere entirely outside of the Huxley–Whiting–Russell triumvirate, as it is a faithful adaptation of a novella (of the same name) by Jarosław Iwaszkiewicz—it appears Huxley's book hadn't even been translated into Polish when Kawalerowicz made his film.

While taking a very different starting position from that of Grandier, Surin also sees his life eventually shattered by Sister Jeanne—in the book (and the film, albeit with slightly different wording), the killer priest orders a wayward nun to return to the convent to tell the mother superior that he did it 'all for her' (Iwaszkiewicz, 1946: 43). Jeanne, the erotomaniac of *The Devils*, is on the receiving end of obsessive love this time around. Although *Mother Joan* and *The Devils* don't have any credited source material in common, they are based on the same span of historical events and do work quite well together, despite their radically different styles. The bulk of Kawalerowicz's film—which references Grandier's death, and in a series of eerie shots you can see the stake at which he died—is austere in the extreme and situates the convent in a remote, desolate wasteland that's a far cry from Russell's cacophonous, cluttered Loudun. Besides the convent, the only locations of note in *Mother Joan* are an inn and some stables, so it's very much a stripped down affair in which Surin's ascetic struggles can be heard with minimal distraction; as a result, it's much closer to Robert Bresson than Ken Russell. It's also a film that's far more interested in the personal, with the political not really figuring—although some have opined that it could be commenting on Poland being sandwiched between the pragmatism of communism and the spiritual conviction of the Church (Townsend, 2005). Perhaps significantly, Kawalerowicz's compatriot Krzysztof Penderecki would also tell the Loudun story in his opera *Die Teufel von Loudun*, based on Whiting's play and written between *Mother Joan* and Russell's film.

While we cannot make any claims that Kawalerowicz's film or the book on which it is based are a direct influence on Russell and his film, the very existence of *Mother Joan of the Angels* did at least demonstrate it was possible to adapt a portion of this most bizarre of stories for the cinema, and Whiting's play served as a conduit which Russell used to get Huxley's book to the screen. *The Devils* stands as a complex adaptation which makes roughly equal use of two extremely fine texts, with the strongest elements of both the book and the play being fused together in remarkable fashion, resulting in a unique and quite visionary piece of cinema. In creating his masterpiece, Ken Russell never lost sight of the message and spirit of Huxley, yet very much depended on the structure and order of Whiting. From Russell's point of view, the book and the play must have enjoyed a symbiotic relationship which provided the most solid of foundations to build on, and it seems fair to speculate that both John Whiting and Aldous Huxley, had they lived for another decade, would have been most impressed with Russell's skilful reshaping of their respective works.

FOOTNOTES

1. The production staged at the 1992 Edinburgh Festival bore the obvious influence of Russell's film, with performances very much modelled on those of Reed, Redgrave, et al.
2. From 1973 to 1980, Brian Murphy played the part of George Roper in *Man About the House* and its spin-off, *George and Mildred*.

Chapter 3: Genre

Nowadays it is common to see *The Devils* lumped in with horror programming, and while identifying the film as belonging to the genre is by no means inaccurate, there's a lot more to say about the film when it comes to classifying it. In many ways, *The Devils* possibly *ends up* as a horror film (as opposed to being designed as one), and the more extreme, graphic elements of the film—as is so often the case—crowd out the other aspects, at least from the general viewer's perspective (and this certainly applied to the general viewer in 1971). But the film very much remains, in essence, as it begins—a historical drama, not being eclipsed by, but rather dovetailing neatly with, its horror elements, which are something of a natural by-product. As such, the largely unnoticed sophistication of the film marked an evolution in screen horror. Rather than setting out to make a horror film (as he clearly did with both his fun Bram Stoker adaptation *The Lair of the White Worm* [1988] and the poorly-received *Gothic* [1986]), or trying to box the film in in terms of genre, Russell simply set about telling his story here, and the genre latterly assigned to *The Devils* appears to be due to its title as much as its content.

A useful comparison point when it comes to examining *The Devils* in terms of genre is another film from the early 1970s, William Friedkin's *The Exorcist*. Widely considered to be one of the finest horror films ever produced, with some claiming it to be the pinnacle of the genre, Friedkin's film and *The Devils* both had Warner Bros. in common, but the American studio took to *The Exorcist* with boundless enthusiasm while recoiling from Russell's film. *The Exorcist*, which was based on William Peter Blatty's best-selling novel, contained a few things already familiar from *The Devils* which, in time, would go on to become horror movie tropes.[1] As mentioned earlier, the events of Loudun are explicitly referenced in Blatty's book:

> *And then those exorcists* … Karras frowned. The exorcists themselves at times became the victims of possession, as had happened in 1634 at the Ursuline Convent of nuns at Loudun, France. Of the four Jesuit exorcists sent there to deal with an epidemic of possession, three […] not only became seemingly possessed, but died soon after. (2011: 241–242)

While the evil on display in *The Devils* is entirely man-made, *The Exorcist* is markedly different in that the evil it depicts lies firmly in the supernatural, which itself helps define the film as 'horror'. Despite the act put on by the nuns in Russell's film, the viewer is at no point led to believe that a demon is behind all this; all we have in *The Devils* are some very real people who inhabit the moral spectrum in various shades of good and evil, whereas in *The Exorcist* there is a very clear line of demarcation between the two concepts. Coming from the standpoint of moral absolutism, *The Exorcist*'s universe is one of God vs. Satan, good vs. bad, right vs. wrong, which makes things reassuringly easy for its audience (and, seemingly, its distributor). It also makes it easier to classify as a horror film, with the two opposing teams in a battle for the spirit making it more easily recognisable as belonging to the genre.

There are also key differences in what each of the directors wants their audiences to invest in the respective stories, and we can take the view that Friedkin very much wants to put his audience in the action and on a specific side. Russell, on the other hand, could be said to be simply presenting these terrible events for us to observe, and an emotional attachment to the protagonist is by no means mandatory as per *The Exorcist*:

> Russell's vision of how events unfold [...] seems intent on giving us a Brechtian sense of detachment, deflecting attention from the real theme of possession. William Friedkin was to view possession in *The Exorcist* slightly differently from the way Ken Russell does in *The Devils*, with Russell eroticising it and Friedkin demonising it. (Bridle, 2004)

Although possession hardly needs any additional demonising and is not the, or even a, 'real theme' (at most, it's a MacGuffin) in *The Devils*—as already mentioned, unlike in *The Exorcist*, at no point is the audience asked to buy into the concept—it is certainly eroticised insofar as the nuns' interpretation of being under a demonic influence is concerned, as their one mode of operating when 'possessed' is to act in as lewd and lascivious a manner as possible. Bridle continues:

> In part, this is why *The Exorcist* has never caused difficulty for audiences or censors in the United States and Russell's film has [....] The question Russell asks of his viewer is not to see his vision as blasphemy, but for us to see what he is portraying as blasphemy. The subtlety is important, since when you see the public blasphemy of the

From left: Jeanne, Barré and Louis are in awe of the blood of Christ.

nuns [...] simultaneously against the private communion of Grandier, the sensitivity of Russell's direction falls into place. (ibid.)

While, as Marc Bridle notes, *The Exorcist* gave US censors no big problems, it was a very different matter in the UK, where its failure to gain a BBFC certificate once the VRA had come into effect led to a full 15 years in the distribution wilderness, at least as far as legal home viewing was concerned. When comparing the two films, there's an obvious irony: while the exorcism in *The Exorcist* purports to be a real one within the framework of a fiction, the one in *The Devils* is a fake one inside a film based on historical fact.[2] The practice of exorcism has always been controversial and is oft debated within and without the Church—at the time of writing, the Catholic Church revealed that the past decade has seen a threefold increase in the amount of exorcisms performed in France ('Booming number', 2017). The idea that exorcism may be a far from altruistic endeavour is an intriguing one:

> With the popularity of Christianity in the Roman Empire, demonic possession became an explanation for erratic behavior in society. Religious men during the Middle Ages practiced exorcisms as a way to imitate Jesus. For instance Saint Francis of Assisi performed an exorcism for a man who had convulsions and foaming from the mouth—a symptom of epilepsy. (Forcen, 2016)

While this lines up fairly well with the exorcism in *The Devils* occurring to explain away the unhinged behaviour of Sister Jeanne, Fernando Espi Forcen's point above is also highly relevant to the film in stating how exorcists looked to copy Christ. The supremely arrogant Father Barré seems to follow this way of thinking, and although he superficially appears to defer to Christ it might well be suspected that he sees himself on at least an equal footing with his saviour; the priest's ostensible attempts to drive out evil spirits add up to little more than extravagant showboating. The title character in *The Exorcist*, on the other hand, is a learned, humble and sincere priest who wishes to serve his lord as much as he wants to rid a young girl of her diabolical predicament. There is no doubt in Fredkin's film as to who's wearing the white hat.

Conversely, *The Devils* works with a form of moral relativism as it asks us to accept a deeply flawed character, one who's created a substantial legacy of bad behaviour, as a type of saint or saviour. You can easily imagine studio executives thinking: *that's* who we're supposed to root for? Additionally, *The Devils* does not show the Catholic Church in a favourable light, whereas in *The Exorcist* the Church and its priests are all that stand between an innocent young girl and the vile demon which threatens to swallow her whole. Incidentally, it's curious that Warners seemed more comfortable with a film in which a child character (although admittedly possessed) spits profanity and masturbates with a key sacramental than they did with *The Devils* and its all-adult victims and perpetrators. This lack of clearly divided sides, as well as apparently being a major turn-off for the studio, is perhaps the main factor in the argument against *The Devils* being viewed as an outright horror film. The lack of a metaphysical aspect also edges the film away from traditional horror, and Barry Keith Grant makes the point that Russell's film 'is an antihorror film, for by demythifying the supernatural it shows the source of horror to be psychological, the result of sexual repression' (2009: 27).

However, it can be argued that the source of horror extends way beyond the psychological, as the State and the Church, both individually and collectively, are the driving forces behind the nightmare which unfolds. Sexual repression merely manifests itself in a form which Grandier's enemies can use to their advantage, and Jeanne's accusations allow for some prime opportunism on the part of those looking to ruin the priest. While it can be hard to extricate the possessed nuns from the machinations of both Church and State, we should remember that if it wasn't a charge of witchcraft that proved to be the death of Grandier, it would most likely have been something equally spurious; the authorities were simply on the lookout for anything on which they could build a case against the priest, and it just so happened that the whole possession drama was the first thing they chanced upon. That said, it's a pretty juicy scandal, and it made for equally fine entertainment for audiences in both the marketplace of seventeenth-century Loudun and the cinemas of twentieth-century London; if a priest was burned as a heretic simply because he was late for confession or used the wrong type of communion wine, the drama would be much reduced. But it's interesting to consider that Russell (nor Huxley nor Whiting before him) didn't embellish or hyperbolate too much in depicting the persecution of Grandier—the farcicality was already there, and the events simply needed to be re-presented to an audience who could see the absurdity in them.

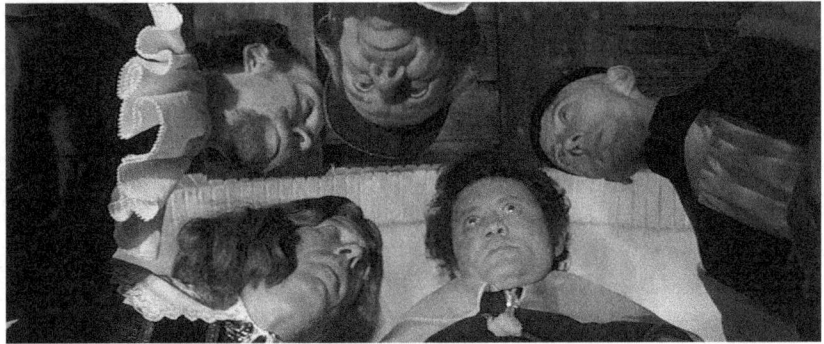

The plot against Grandier gets underway.

Perhaps many years of dry, dusty historical dramas had conditioned 1971 audiences as to what constituted such a film, and those who'd snoozed through Ken Hughes' *Cromwell* (1970) and its ilk were certainly alert when Russell took them on an unexpectedly wild tour of seventeeth-century France. *The Devils*, despite the trail blazed by the aforementioned *Witchfinder General*, made a poor fit for such a label. Additionally, the title—which pitches the film somewhere between a Dennis Wheatley novel and Hammer's *The Witches* (1966)—surely indicates that this is a horror film? There is no big problem with categorising *The Devils* as a historical drama-cum-horror, but the film is also an inadvertent genre-hopping exercise which could also be described as a love story, or even a political thriller, of sorts (post-Vietnam, of course, the 1970s would become the decade of the political thriller).

Just as T. S. Eliot's J. Alfred Prufrock was said to have measured out his life with coffee spoons, it could be suggested that a certain type of horror fan ascertains the level of their devotion via a mental checklist of show-stoppingly gory moments: the skewered eyeball of *Zombi 2* (1979), the murder of Jane in *Tenebrae* (1982), the piano wire amputation of *Audition* (1999), and so on. Many horror films, classic and otherwise, feature *that* scene, during which the viewer will either avert their gaze or endure—the second option taken by those wishing to earn another stripe. But this oft-courted notoriety frequently comes at a price for filmmakers—such a scene can define a film to the extent that the rest of the running time is eclipsed by that one shocking moment. Which is great if you're after several million views on YouTube; not so good if you'd like people to remember, or maybe even extract some meaning from, your entire work.

Thankfully, *The Devils*—at least in any of its officially released versions—is not a film which can be distilled into one gasp-inducing clip (although chapter 6 will highlight how it came perilously close to featuring such a scene, before serendipity stepped in). The film is graphic, but more in terms of sex and nudity than violence. As regards gore, the two most extreme scenes in the film are Grandier's torture and subsequent burning—with the latter being the tougher watch. Even the torture scene, in which Father Barré gleefully smashes Grandier's legs, is one that sees its overall effect achieved more through implication. While we do glimpse the end product of the torture in the form of Grandier's mangled lower limbs, we are spared the moments when hammer hits bone—and we don't actually need to witness these, as the violence is all there in Barré's face, with some fine editing making us feel as if we've seen far more than we actually have. While the climactic burning scene—which features some excellent make-up work—provides a more unflinching look at Grandier's ordeal, it still does nothing to diminish what has preceded it. In a lesser film, the execution of Grandier would be singled out as the big moment, but in the context of *The Devils* it has an air of the quotidian; it serves the narrative, and simply fits in where it could very easily have stood out.

In this respect, *The Devils* shares much with *The Texas Chain Saw Massacre* (1974). Tobe Hooper's seminal horror film has a vaguely cartoonish—and, if we're honest, censor-baiting—title which would appear to telegraph wall-to-wall mayhem and bloodshed à la H. G. Lewis, yet there's little in the way of explicit violence on show. The most squirm-inducing moment comes when horror icon-elect Leatherface impales the unfortunate (and very much alive) Pam on a meat hook; it's a sickening, horrifying moment, but by no means a graphic one, and its grim effectiveness—which is inversely proportionate to its explicitness—is on a par with the torture scene in *The Devils*. Over the many decades since its release, Hooper's film has proved initially disappointing to many a gorehound, as it almost certainly fails to live down to the pulpy promise of its grindhouse-friendly title. However, subsequent viewings of the movie—once audiences have managed to get over the paucity of chainsaw action—reveal a film drenched in a feverish dread which seeps way beyond the margins of any and all unpleasant acts which may be featured. This is largely what has cemented the film's classic status, and, as with *The Devils*, there is no single 'go-to' scene which can be readily fast-forwarded to; those in search of horror's greatest hits will need to look elsewhere for their quick fix.

It is worth considering that both *The Devils* and *The Texas Chain Saw Massacre* confounded the censors for much the same reason; analysing the latter, James Rose observes how 'the film was, to some extent, censor-proof because it was not *individual* scenes that needed exorcising but the overarching *feel* of the film' (2013: 21). In a description which could just as easily have been referencing *The Devils*, the BBFC noted that Hooper's film conjured 'an atmosphere of madness, threat and impeding [sic] violence, whilst shying away from showing much in the way of explicit detail ('The Texas Chain Saw Massacre', n.d.). In the case of *The Texas Chain Saw Massacre*, the BBFC simply cut the Gordian knot and suppressed the film for quarter of a century, whereas while the alterations the board demanded for *The Devils* (see chapter 6) resulted in a releasable film, they could not change the inherent nature of the work; the very essence of these films presented problems which, somewhat ironically, no amount of hacking or slashing could solve. As Ida Arnold put it in Graham Greene's classic novel *Brighton Rock*: 'It's like those sticks of rock: bite it all the way down, you'll still read Brighton' (1938: 291).

Mapping the fault lines in these films is no easy task for viewers—be they censors, critics or the paying public. You can watch *The Devils* in any of its versions, yet no matter how much violence (such as it is) or nudity is trimmed, the same disconcerting background thrum runs throughout the film, the same entropic nature is evident, and, as with *The Texas Chain Saw Massacre*, it's the general *feel* of the work which nags and gnaws away at the viewer. A film such as the aforementioned *Zombi 2* offered relatively few censorial headaches—simply excise some of the more extreme moments, which is exactly what the BBFC did in 1980, and the film could be freely exhibited. Films infinitely more graphic than *Texas Chain Saw* have sailed past the BBFC—which seems very tough on Hooper's movie, given that it contains 'no explicit sexual element [...] and relatively little visible violence' ('Texas Chainsaw', 1999, as cited in Rose, 2013: 25). Tone, it would seem, is far more troubling to censors than overt sex or violence—both of which can usually be quarantined and removed, leaving the rest of a work uncontaminated.

While there's little doubt that *Texas Chain Saw* is a *horror* film, *The Devils* occupies a significantly more opaque space as far as genre is concerned, but what can be said with some certainty is that the tone and mood set by Russell's film place it firmly in the category of *shocking* films, and as such it is perhaps a movie the viewing public should be more wary of—more so than films merely containing copious amounts of violence and gore. There are other problematic films which fall into the same murky category as *The Devils*, including *The Black Panther* (1977), *Angst* (1983) and *Snowtown* (2011), all of which are concerned with multiple murderers. As with both *The Devils* and *Texas Chain Saw*, these three films are based (to varying extents) on grim real-life events, which may be seen as a contributing factor to the unnerving, bleak mood they create; nomenclature issues aside, these films are certainly more horrific than many readily identifiable 'horror' films, and any attempt to edit any of them into something more palatable is a fool's errand. Moreover, each of these films gives off a miasma which completely distracts from any and all graphic content which may be in evidence—the opposite of the film which trails in the wake of its big gruesome moment.

Another, much more obvious example of such a film, one which also takes inspiration from true crimes, is John McNaughton's *Henry: Portrait of a Serial Killer* (1986), a *sui generis* exploitation-Cassavetes hybrid anchored by an almost suffocating sense of oppressiveness—albeit one that's very slightly offset by the moments of juddering violence which punctuate proceedings. But that *Henry* lacks a defining scene of bloodshed is testament to the queasy power which emanates from every frame. BBFC cuts to McNaughton's film seem to have been made on a rather arbitrary, token level—presumably a pre-emptive move which would allow the board to defend itself by saying that the work did not get through the classification process unscathed, even if the malevolent spirit which inhabited the film remained essentially undisturbed by such tinkering. To an extent, the same rationale appears to have been applied 20 years earlier (*Henry* wasn't submitted until 1991) when the BBFC passed *The Devils*.

It is reasonable to say that *Snowtown*, *Henry*, *Angst* and *The Black Panther* are all non-horror films, yet they have consistently proved to be of serious interest to those who consider themselves horror fans. This is not simply because murder is a key feature in each of these movies, but rather that they all share an unstable, volatile nature which can't be easily shaken off by the viewer; such qualities cannot be conveyed by straightforward synopses. What constitutes a 'horror' film is, of course, all rather subjective, but it is notable that there are films out there which don't obviously belong to the genre, yet are sought out by horror fans. Given the way in which the genre is often derided and dismissed by many, it's pleasing to know that some enthusiasts of horror cinema aren't so myopic when it comes to seeking out interesting and challenging works which can, after a fashion, be co-opted into becoming associate members of the genre.

So, if we are able to conclude that horror is to be found in many films which operate outside of the generally accepted confines of the genre, with *The Devils* being a case in point, how do we then define Russell's film's relationship to the genre in a wider sense? On paper, it could be argued that the film's easily recognisable horror elements (demonic possession, witch hunts, torture, the plague, a hideously violent death, and so on) mark it as an easy sell as a piece of genre cinema—and, it must also be said, make it all sound rather rote. A Hammer or Blumhouse quickie could just as easily incorporate all of these elements and result in a film which is categorically horror yet lacks the needling atmosphere of Russell's film. If the basic ingredients are more or less the same, why does *The Devils* seem to amount to something which greatly exceeds what might reasonably be expected? The difference, I think, lies in the film's connective tissue—what binds this whole iconoclastic work together is infinitely more important than any given scene or action, or indeed anything that is *seen*. Or, to put it another way, while the film's individual components may function perfectly well in isolation, *The Devils* is simply *wired wrong*.

If the form and content of the film don't prove to be sufficiently off-putting for the general viewer, *The Devils* has an unfortunate blot on its production history which may have also contributed to its status as a movie best avoided. It has been claimed that some of the nude female extras (and even a few of the main performers) were subjected to assaults during the filming of some of the more chaotic crowd scenes (Crouse, 2012). These allegations, while neither new nor high-profile, feel especially disconcerting in the present day; with the 2017 birth of the #MeToo movement, the genie's well and truly out of the bottle regarding sexual harassment/assault in the film industry. Reports of on-set impropriety during *The Devils*' shoot makes the film even less digestible for audiences who, in a post-Weinstein world, are acutely aware of countless other, similar accusations.

Russell is not widely regarded as a director of horror films, and the eclectic nature of his body of work really resists such pigeonholing. His influence on the genre, outside of the few films he made that could be termed as horror, has largely gone unnoticed, yet John Kenneth Muir has explored how Russell influenced much of the successful horror output of the 1980s, such as *A Nightmare on Elm Street* (1984) and *Hellraiser* (1987), both of which led to long-running franchises:

> [F]or a magical span in the 1980s, Russell's penchant for hallucinatory imagery seemed to closely align with commercial interests and with a commercial genre at its blazing apex (before a horror retraction and recession looming in the 1990s). What horror fans are left with from this fateful conjunction are two of the most colorful and flamboyant examples of the form, ones that serve as time capsules for the beginning and end of the Reagan/Thatcher era and that remind us of how a good idea can become (intentionally) ridiculous in light of multitudinous repetition. (2009: 193)

The two films Muir is referencing are *Altered States* (1980) and *The Lair of the White Worm*, which effectively top and tail Russell's career in the 1980s and sandwich a glut of horror films which were often lurid, sometimes inventive, and frequently profitable. It is a perceptive point that Russell helped set up 80s horror and returned to see it off with a most tongue-in-cheek effort which critiques and parodies the way in which the genre had become tired, stale and formulaic. Between these films Russell had, of course, turned out *Gothic* (perhaps his most readily identifiable horror film, but still only a moderate success), but it seems a pity that the filmmaker who was there for the opening and closing of this particular chapter in genre cinema history didn't receive anything like the financial rewards reaped by the franchises and style of film he had a small part in launching. Russell's 1980s horror titles (*Crimes of Passion*, with a typecast Anthony Perkins, is also fair game for this list) were all imaginative, resourceful films which deserved to be seen more widely, but perhaps a lack of branding—Russell lacked the genre clout of say, Lucio Fulci or Dario Argento, nor were his films in this period part of a series—got in the way of them being marketed to their full potential.

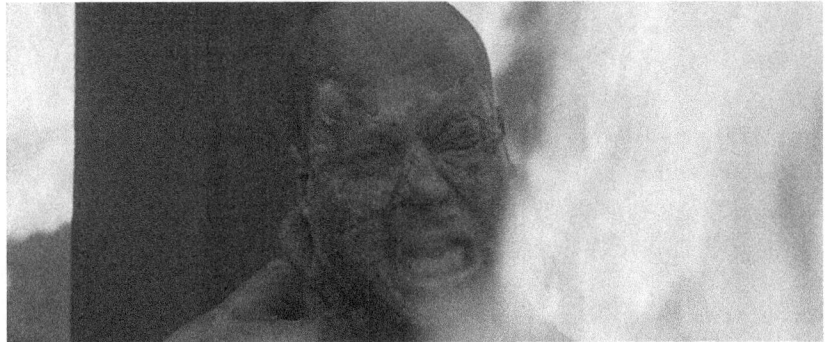

Grandier burns at the stake.

All of which leaves *The Devils* as a film that may well have found a place in the horror genre in retrospect—at the time of its release, there were no horror films in Russell's filmography, nor would there be any more for the remainder of the decade. In its day, and for the rest of the 1970s, there was no real reason or incentive for anyone to classify the film as belonging to the horror genre—Russell's work in that period was already frequently considered extreme, grotesque, flamboyant, edgy and horrifying, but it was the headline-grabbing sex and/or nudity which would subsequently inform public perception. *The Devils* had plenty of naked flesh on display, as did Pier Paolo Pasolini's *The Decameron* (1970)—a picaresque tale in which lusty priest Grandier wouldn't look especially out of place—and both films provided a more acceptable way in which to view screen sex: as part of legitimate stories (based on prestigious literary works, no less) and away from the stigma of 'adults only' cinema. The idea of explicit sexual material effectively being laundered as it takes its place in serious fictional narrative is certainly one that's both endured and developed in the decades since *The Devils* first appeared. This aspect, combined with the scenes of violence and torture which were also present, certainly makes the film marketable as a particular kind of horror—albeit one which wasn't too familiar to Anglophone audiences, as the work of the likes of Jess Franco and Jean Rollin wasn't (and never became) part of the vocabulary of the mainstream cinemagoer in English-speaking countries.

The Devils, of course, initially received wide distribution and was thrust on an unsuspecting audience lacking any meaningful reference point for categorising the film. It's much easier now, when considering Russell's later horror works and the European exploitation films which both preceded and succeeded it, to find a place for *The Devils* in the context of cinema history, but that it wasn't broadly identified as a horror film at the time is rather telling; the years of screen horror have allowed us, somewhat reductively, to identify the film as belonging to the genre, but we shouldn't let what followed obfuscate the complex nature of Russell's unique creation.

FOOTNOTES

1. *The Exorcist*'s famed spider-walking sequence—only included in the film since the extended version was released in 2000—is one of several specific features Friedkin's film shares with *The Devils*. A confoundingly bizarre aspect of the BFI DVD of *The Devils* is to be found in the English subtitle stream, where the spider-walking Sister Jeanne's explanation for not speaking Latin—'I haven't travelled much'—has been rendered as 'I am a travelling monkey'; as mondegreens go, this has to be one of the more spectacular examples. Spider-walking can also be seen in *Mother Joan of the Angels* and Bruno Dumont's Joan of Arc film *Jeannette, l'enfance de Jeanne d'Arc* (2017).
2. Blatty's novel and screenplay were said to be inspired by a real-life case involving a young boy known only as 'Roland Doe'. The film makes no onscreen claims to be based on historical fact (an all persons fictitious disclaimer is present in the end credits), and is hardly unusual in being a fiction which takes inspiration from recorded events.

Chapter 4: Themes

A key message in *The Devils*, which creeps up on us rather subtly, given Ken Russell's rather unjust reputation as a sledgehammer of a director, concerns the misery and destruction which can result when politics and religion jump into bed together. As the film's final, spectacular shot reveals the ruins of the magnificent city walls shown (equally spectacularly) near the start of the film, the scale of the horror of what's occurred really resonates; these bookends chillingly convey the film's main point. It's Cardinal Richelieu's desire to build a new, centralised (and Protestant-free) France in which, as he puts it to Louis XIII in the extravagant, unnerving opening scene, 'Church and State are one' which has led to the destroyed walls of Loudun we see at the end, and it's clear to see who has blood on their hands. As mentioned earlier, Russell said *The Devils* was his only political film, and you can just about taste his revulsion at the unholy marriage that's occurred between Church and State; the film presents a compelling argument for the separation of the two entities, which eventually came to pass in France in 1905.

There's also a much narrower focus at work within this broader scheme of political shenanigans, as we witness Urbain Grandier, the film's main character, undergo the transformation from sinner to saint (of sorts). Grandier is an arrogant, promiscuous and politically influential priest who, as someone who cherishes his city's autonomy, proves to be the fly in the ointment for Richelieu, yet his unorthodox ways make him easy meat for the Cardinal. Richelieu and his agents use religion to cast Grandier as a heretic, but the real motives (and ramifications) are political—as such, Grandier, just like Joan of Arc two centuries earlier, is actually a political heretic burned as a religious one. Eventually robbed of the swagger he possesses in the film's early scenes, Grandier gradually finds humility, true love, and comes to peace with God, whom he connects with on a personal level largely devoid of the systems employed by the Catholic Church he's served for so long. That the Church can be bypassed—which firmly goes against St. Augustine's idea that 'you cannot have God as your Father unless you have the Church as your Mother'—is a subtle yet daring facet of Russell's film; what's especially sophisticated is that Russell suggests we get past this agent of misery instead of viewing it as a dead end. In *The Devils*, the Church is seen to actually block access to God—the polar opposite of its stated intention.

In a rare moment of quiet, Urbain Grandier prays to God.

This most sincere aspect of the film tapped into an idea which was becoming more prevalent in the early 1970s and has grown ever stronger since—that anyone wishing to find God may, or even *must*, make that connection on their own terms. Dismissing Angela Merici's book as 'sanctimonious claptrap', Grandier goes on to make the valid point to Madeleine that 'most religions believe that by crying "Lord! Lord!" often enough they can contrive to enter the kingdom of Heaven'.[1] Radical stuff, and Grandier clearly understands how beliefs can be mistaken for faith; most of his parishioners could be considered to *believe* in God and may observe every necessary protocol and ritual, but belief can be both objective and detached. Faith, on the other hand and in this context, requires a personal connection to Christ which requires little to none of the religious scaffolding which is in place for mere belief to exist. However, in *The Devils* it appears the telephone doesn't work both ways; Russell's vision of Loudun appears to be more aligned with a deist view—the God in whom priest and populace place their faith and/or belief doesn't intervene as Grandier burns and Laubardemont triumphs.

Of course, it's quite understandable that the Church wouldn't want it to be spread around that one can independently maintain a relationship with God— much like a baker is unlikely to encourage people to make their own bread. While it should be noted that Grandier's treatment by the Church in *The Devils* is not quotidian, it is nonetheless at the limits of a spectrum in which the opposite end sees the institution— in any denomination—frequently fail to put its messages of compassion, inclusiveness and forgiveness into action. In terms of spirituality, it may be that Grandier is having his cake and eating it, but it is hard to argue with his philosophy when one witnesses the stifling *modus operandi* of the institution he represents.

In daring to suggest that organised religion may not be the best route to take, Russell again lays himself open to lazy accusations of blasphemy and sacrilege. Yet there's an authentic and heartfelt yearning for spirituality at the core of Grandier, the film, and, by extension, its director. On this basis, *The Devils* has some common interests with *The Exorcist*, even if the latter wholeheartedly endorses personal faith and the institution that is the Church. Russell would later unsubscribe from the teachings of organised religion as the need to nourish his soul took him off in other directions (Russell, 1989: 194). While the message may be over-amplified in the film, the need to separate Christ's teachings from those who have distorted them—while appointing themselves God's ambassadors on Earth—was clearly seen as a pressing one; the film's criticism of Richelieu, Barré and co. applies to any and all who look to shape Jesus' message for their own gain. In *The Devils*, organised religion is depicted, not for the first or last time, as a mechanism to control the ignorant masses, all of whom are deemed vastly inferior by and to the great and good who run the Church. The clergy form a sort of ruling class who seem to relish lording over the people, and there's little humility in evidence among Church officials who see themselves as operating on a completely different plane from the townsfolk of Loudun.

Cardinal Richelieu himself is seen to possess an all-consuming, unshakeable desire to persecute Protestants—because they're culturally different, not because they don't believe in purgatory; in Huxley's book, it's qualified as 'and anyhow they were heretics' (1952: 61). The whole transubstantiation-consubstantiation debate is evidently not one in which the Cardinal and his pettifogging underlings have much interest, and Richelieu appears to greatly favour matters of state over any ecclesiastical duties he may have. Unlike in Maurice Pialat's stunning Palme d'Or winner *Under the Sun of Satan* (*Sous le soleil de Satan*, 1987) and its 1926 Georges Bernanos source novel, no one here is involved in a mighty ascetic battle, nor rises to what Janet Maslin, reviewing Pialat's masterpiece, referred to as 'a stunning test of faith' (1987). Loudun may be steeped in tradition, but, as Huxley states, is effectively a spiritual wasteland:

> Of the existence at Loudun, during the parson's incumbency, of any genuinely spiritual

religion there is no evidence. Widespread concern with the spiritual life arises only in the neighborhood of exceptional individuals who know by direct experience that God is a Spirit and must be worshiped in spirit. (1952: 12)

Tellingly, the main theological points in the film are raised via Grandier, a character who is seen to actively re-evaluate his relationship with God over the course of the film, and in the end opts for the direct line approach described by Huxley above. With his faith rewired and streamlined, there's something very refreshing about witnessing Grandier connect with God without much need for monstrances, thuribles and crucifixes—all things which, it would seem, have actually hindered his spiritual growth. Russell, through Grandier, shows us that knowing the catechism and knowing God are by no means the same thing. In the end, as Grandier is beaten, bloodied, and burned at the stake, it's hard not to have sympathy for a man who's steadfastly improved as all around him has turned to dust. It can be argued that Grandier only becomes a better man once he's been backed into a corner, although it could be countered that how one ends their life is more important than how one begins it, and Grandier dies with his integrity intact.

The crowds enjoy the spectacle of Grandier's death.

Interestingly, the film doesn't really appear to be too hard on organised religion (although Russell, someone with firsthand experience of Roman Catholicism, brilliantly essays the theatre of the Church), but rather focuses on the ways in which it can be (mis)used for political expedience.[2] A perhaps seldom-considered function of the Church is obvious in the film, and is discussed in Huxley's book:

> Nature abhors a vacuum, even in the mind. Today the aching void of boredom is filled and perpetually renewed by movies and radio, television and the comic strips. More fortunate than we, or else less fortunate (who knows?), our ancestors depended, for the assuagement of their ennui, on the weekly performances of their parish priest, supplemented from time to time by the discourses of visiting Capuchins or travelling Jesuits. (1952: 25)

It's the hand in glove way in which Church and State operate which most troubles Russell and Grandier, and the chilling scene in which Grandier's file is pulled from a huge archive behind double doors emblazoned with a large red cross marks the Church out as the STASI of its day (Dee, 2012). The religious aspects—notably the faked demonic possession of an order of nuns—are portrayed simply as a means for political ends, as Richelieu knows that setting up Grandier as a nun-corrupting sorcerer will help clear the path for his plan to defortify the city. The carefree, decadent King Louis—who alleviates boredom by murdering Huguenot prisoners who are dressed as blackbirds—acts as if he doesn't have a dog in this fight, and his playful exposing of the demonic possessions as a sham affects the outcome not one jot, further emphasising who really holds the keys to power (why does no-one question the—admittedly fleeting—power of the empty box Louis wields?). We can also touch upon contemporary issues here—just as Richelieu uses a case of supposed mass possession to gain political leverage, some opponents of the 2003 invasion of Iraq felt the instigators had ulterior motives, and that both the *casus belli* and the legality of the war should have been brought into question.[3]

It is easy to watch *The Devils* and think, just as the film was a groundbreaking effort, that the events depicted were somehow novel for seventeenth-century France. As Urbain Grandier points out early on in the film, the religious wars had ended before this story begins, but during the decades when the war was raging, the Catholic Church seemed quite willing to use displays of exorcism as a way in which to help subjugate the enemy:

> A famous case in 1566 was that of Nicole Obry, a newly married Catholic sixteen-year-old French girl [….] The demon Beelzebub talked trough [sic] Nicole's mouth; he claimed that the Protestant Huguenots were his friends […] [and] she was fed with several hosts until the demons came out of her body. This public exorcism was an attack against the Protestant Huguenots who questioned the dogma of

transubstantiation. Many Huguenots returned to Catholicism, whereas others realized that the whole performance was a trick by the Catholic Church to confirm the dogma and attack its rivals. (Forcen, 2016)

This dog and pony show appears to have been quite an effective one, as not only Laon (where the Obry exorcism took place) but Loudun saw large numbers of Protestants convert to Catholicism in the wake of the supposed possessions; that these occurrences took place roughly 70 years apart demonstrates how sustained the Catholic Church's campaign was. While the religious wars may have officially ended as the sixteenth century came to a close, the events at Loudun prove that this particular battle, as waged by the Catholic Church, rumbled on for many decades. Grandier's death and the destruction of the city walls, although significant events, pale against the grand scale of the centrepiece of the religious wars that was the St. Bartholomew's Day massacre of 1572, and what occurred in Loudun could be more readily explained away as isolated incidents caused by a troublesome priest.[4] Given that Grandier was Catholic, it meant the Church could neatly avoid accusations of persecution—although the inclusive priest's death was the first in a chain of events which would rapidly see Loudun's Huguenots at the mercy of both Church and State, whose stances ranged from unsympathetic (at best) to downright hostile.

The Devils was released decades before the eruption of multiple scandals regarding sexual abuse within the Catholic Church, and had such cases been at the forefront of the news in the early 1970s it would have been impossible to view the film as anything other a savage attack on the institution. Sexual abuse doesn't really figure too prominently in the film (or perhaps it's eclipsed), although most will consider the brutal, highly invasive public exorcism of Sister Jeanne to be classed as such—while it's the chemist and the surgeon who do the most interfering with Jeanne, the ritual is directed by the Church and overseen by one of their priests. Huxley memorably notes that 'Barré had treated her to an experience that was the equivalent, more or less, of a rape in a public lavatory' (1952: 115). In the film, the same priest later declares: 'The exorcisms have failed. We must resort to other measures', then proceeds to remove his cloak and, in full predator mode, descends onto the bed on which Jeanne is convalescing following her suicide attempt. The camera does not follow Barré, but stays with a reaction shot of Father Mignon, whose wide-eyed expression—coupled with the grunts and moans coming from the bed, as Barré breathlessly recites the Trinitarian formula—leaves the viewer in little doubt as to what such 'other measures' entail. The dehumanisation and objectification of Jeanne is relayed by Huxley in a manner which crushes the soul in its depiction of an abuser at work:

> And now [...] she was in the hands of the egregious M. Barré. The phantasy of a downward self-transcendence had been transformed into the brute fact of his actually treating her as something [...] fit only to be bawled at, manipulated, sent by reiterated suggestion into fits and finally subjected, against what remained of her will and in spite of the remnants of her modesty, to the outrage of a forcible colonic irrigation. (ibid.)

Father Barré.

While such activity was not considered synonymous with the Catholic Church in 1971, contemporary viewers may well pick up on Barré's treatment of Jeanne as correlating with what we now know to be a far greater, wider problem. The issue has been covered in recent years in films including *Doubt* (2008), of which former Catholic priest Daniel S. Cutrara writes:

> He [Father Flynn] is a progressive priest inspired by the ideals of Vatican II and reaching out to the community. His nemesis, Sister Aloysius, however, is the archetypal authoritarian nun whom generations of Catholic schoolchildren have learned to fear. When Flynn begins to pay special attention to the only African-American boy [...] in the school, he becomes the target of Sister Aloysius's investigation. Flynn likens the investigation to a witch hunt that ruins careers, and the priest becomes an object of sympathy for the audience. (2014: 206)

The above description contains much in common with *The Devils*, and although *Doubt* eventually goes down a very different path from Russell's film and is overtly concerned with sexual abuse, it is striking to see the superficial similarities which exist between the two films. After viewing *Doubt*, it is likely that one could then see *The Devils* as referring to sexual abuse in the Church, and possibly even signposting—by accident or design—something which would be uncovered in years to come. Similarly, *Spotlight* (2015)—a rare breed in being one of the few watchable Best Picture Oscar-winners of the twenty-first century so far—digs deep into the Catholic Church sexual abuse scandal, and is a movie which sharpens the senses when re-viewing pre-scandal works including *The Devils*.

Likewise, Conrad Black's mammoth encomium of Québec premier Maurice Duplessis, published in the late 1970s, takes on a very different slant when you consider the subsequent campaign of the Duplessis Orphans, who, like the Russell of *The Devils*, were in no doubt that both Church and State had colluded with horrifying results.[5] At the beginning of *Duplessis* there's a description which could just as well apply to Russell's Loudun, as the author depicts Duplessis' hometown of Trois-Rivières as 'a rugged and traditional community. Its massive stone buildings symbolized the stern, watchful, immutable supremacy of the Church' (Black, 1977: 9). Furthermore, Black notes how the Québec Church 'essentially believed in the paramountcy of Church over state' (1977: 10). The parallels with the France of *The Devils* (despite its supposed Gallicanism) are startling, and, as with its mother country in the early twentieth century, post-Duplessis Québec eventually managed a separation of Church and State as the ministries of Education and Health were prised from the Church's grasp during the *Révolution tranquille* of the 1960s.

For both the Duplessis Orphans and Urbain Grandier in their respective times and places, this schism was, sadly, too late in coming. If *The Devils* can be said to comment on sexual abuse within the Church, then it would seem that the film telegraphs something from both the 1600s and the 1970s which would only come out into the open once both eras were firmly in the past. It is, of course, easy to use hindsight to view something from a very different angle and to graft additional meaning, but there is something in *The Devils* concerning sexual abuse and the Church which goes way beyond a subjective reading. As already mentioned, perhaps the surrounding chaos in the film enabled this relatively subtle aspect to go unnoticed; in a less busy movie, Barré's treatment of Jeanne would stand out much more. As Jeanne's showcase exorcism descends into chaos, Rangier, a watching hotelier, hollers 'these priests are depraved'. Back in 1971, such a line would have been considered throwaway, maybe even absurd—nowadays, many will feel a real sense of discomfort during this moment as they reflect on the revelations of recent years.

Irony tends to be lost on those who deserve it the most, and anyone who saw to get on their high horse about *The Devils* will doubtless have missed that the film highlights the perils of narrow-mindedness. Russell was always up against it as he wrapped a serious message in graphic content; a full frontal will always usurp a hermeneutical debate, after all, and most of the film's opponents were in no mood to attempt to decode anything that may have lain beyond the film's depiction of nudity, blasphemy and torture. While the film has much to say regarding power, corruption and lies at the highest level, in a way its lessons can't, or rather won't, be learned by those most in need of them. In *The Devils* Ken Russell discusses both politics *and* religion, and knows exactly who he'll offend—the trouble is, those who could really benefit from what Russell imparts will either switch off or walk out. A particularly pessimistic message conveyed by the film is that those running the show will do just as they please, for good or ill. Just as with the Coens' *No Country For Old Men* (2007), the pervasive feeling is that evil will always win out, and as the flames lick around Urbain Grandier, the inevitability of the outcome is both horrifying and depressing.

FOOTNOTES

1. Merici founded the Company of St. Ursula in 1535, and was made a saint in 1807. In *The Devils*, her book is given to Madeleine by Sister Jeanne after the former has expressed a desire to join the convent.
2. Russell was a practising Roman Catholic when he filmed *The Devils*, having converted to the faith from his Church of England upbringing.
3. The reason given was that Iraq was developing and storing chemical, biological and nuclear 'weapons of mass destruction'. Despite more than 18 months of detailed inspections, no evidence of such weapons was found.

4. Some useful background on the religious wars—which get little exposition in *The Devils*—can be found in Patrice Chereau's excellent film *La Reine Margot* (1994), which focuses on the first wife of Louis XIII's father (Medori, 2013).
5. Duplessis' two periods as premier of Québec are collectively known as the *Grande Noirceur* (Great Darkness), times in which many of the province's orphanages were reclassified as psychiatric institutions so as to receive greater funding from the Canadian government. Roughly 20,000 children were falsely certified as having mental illnesses and were placed in Church-run homes where emotional, physical and sexual abuse were all commonplace. In the 1990s, the Duplessis Orphans began a campaign against the Church and government responsible for their ill treatment.

Chapter 5: Gender and Sexuality

The Devils could never be described as coy in any way, but in terms of gender and sexuality it does possess, at its core, a very traditional outlook that, dare it be said, is quite a good fit with the philosophies of many of those responsible for the film's critical opprobrium. Our protagonist, Grandier, is a red-blooded male and apparently a heartthrob for the majority of Loudun's female population. As he's being tortured in the film's latter stages, Grandier confesses, 'I have been a man. I have loved women', clearly seeing the two things as being concordant. This statement also serves to further emasculate Louis XIII, who has exited the film by this stage and will be discussed presently.

More problematically, there are numerous female characters in *The Devils*, and the bulk of them are defined through their relationships to/with the louche Grandier—most are in love/lust with the priest and/or driven hysterical by him. *The Aurum Film Encyclopaedia: Horror* goes as far as to accuse the Russell of *The Devils* as having 'virulent contempt for women' (Hardy, 1996, as cited in Black, 1999). The curmudgeonly Leslie Halliwell, meanwhile, considered the film to be 'a pointless pantomime for misogynists' (1986: 252). Regardless of where they stand on the Grandier spectrum, one thing all these women have in common is that they are infantilised through their relationships with/to the priest: the pouting Phillipe, with her ringlets, pancake make-up and green lipstick, is depicted as a spoiled child who has the temerity to bother Grandier with the pregnancy he's responsible for; the gauche Madeleine is submissive, ineffectual and unappealing; and the apt to bolt Jeanne, a beautiful woman with severe kyphosis, is shown to be driven completely mad by lust. Whether fantasising about Grandier-as-Christ or giving in to her onanistic urges in clear view of one of her equally sex-starved charges, Jeanne is a hysteric whose happiness completely depends on the feelings of a man she's never even met. Such is the Grandier effect.

In *The Devils of Loudun*, Aldous Huxley contextualises the importance of sex to social standing—at least from a male viewpoint—in the France of the time:

Sister Jeanne chides her charges.

> The conquest of a celebrated beauty was equivalent, very nearly, to the conquest of a province. For their triumphs in the boudoir and the bed, such men as Marsillac and Nemours and the Chevalier de Grammont enjoyed a fame almost equal, while it lasted, to that of Gustavus Adolphus or Wallenstein. (1952: 34)

This helps us understand why Grandier, as we first encounter him in the film, confidently struts around the city streets. While he may possess interim governing powers in Loudun, it's his more permanent role as serial seducer of the city's women which gives him his peacock-like demeanour. He immediately follows up his 'I have loved women' statement mentioned above with 'I have enjoyed power'; just as we are meant to link his earlier statement of being a man with loving women, it appears that the latter is also tied to his perception of dominance. This certainly ties in with Huxley's statement regarding status being in line with sexual conquests, and the author goes on to say, with no lack of humour:

> Sex can be used either for self-affirmation or for self-transcendence—either to intensify the ego [...] or else to annihilate the *persona* [....] With his [Grandier's] peasant girls and his middle-class widows of little scruple and large appetite, the parson could get all the self-transcendence he wanted. (ibid.)

As a side note, it is interesting that Huxley yet again flags self-transcendence, as that stage eventually became the capstone in Maslow's hierarchy of needs. Writing in a style which wouldn't look at all out of place in Huxley, Maslow claimed that '[t]ranscendence refers to the very highest and most inclusive or holistic levels of human consciousness' (1971: 269). While the above quote from Huxley is more a joke regarding Grandier's sexual proclivities than a serious exploration of anything Maslow may have theorised in his career, the author unwittingly draws attention to how the work of the renowned psychologist at least lines up with, if not informs, the thinking in *The Devils of Loudun*. While Huxley brought up the concept of self-transcendence before Maslow amended his model to include it, many of the book's philosophical arguments appear to have been influenced by the five-tier pyramid Maslow sketched out way back in 1943.

Grandier himself is seen as someone who can enjoy carnal relations out of wedlock while maintaining a relationship with God (although the strength of his faith only fully emerges as the story progresses). It is notable that Grandier is able to do both of these things while remaining a sane, functioning adult—in fact, Grandier may well be the most reasonable and well-adjusted character in the film. None of the female characters—with the possible exception of Madeleine—are able to juggle sex and faith, at least not with any success. That sex and religion make for uncomfortable bedfellows is seen through the way in which the convent's occupants become unhinged when sexual thoughts are encountered; it starts from the top down, with Sister Jeanne leading by example as her lusty thoughts of Grandier consume what apparently little sanity she has left. In his book *Wicked Cinema: Sex and Religion on Screen*, Daniel S. Cutrara writes:

> The depictions of these dichotomies generally reveal the irrationality of the believer's relationship with his/her God. How the believer negotiates the competing demands of spirit/flesh and reason/faith marks him/her as different from the secular norm. For example, those who possess faith are depicted as having to reject reason. A common trope in film and television is the religious girl who is torn between her sexual desire and maintaining her virginity. Her religious belief tells her that being a virgin is good and gives her a spiritual purity, whereas her sexual desire is of the flesh and bad. (2014: 208)

This accurately sums up the nuns of *The Devils*. While, as we'll touch on in a moment, few of them seem to have entered the convent on the basis of a genuine spiritual calling, the nuns have nonetheless been conditioned by the teachings of the Church and associated concepts of purity and impurity. It is notable that when an out of control Jeanne—clawing at the face and hair of the newly-married Madeleine—spits insults including 'whore', 'fornicator', 'seducer', and, most memorably, 'sacrilegious bitch', her unbridled rage does not permit her to extend beyond using Church-friendly terminology ('bitch' aside), which one feels she would use at this moment were an arsenal of profanity at her disposal.[1] In the play, Barré claims Jeanne's 'degraded imagination and filthy language [...] cannot spring unaided from a cloistered woman' (Whiting, 1961: 59). This makes for a rare occasion when Barré says something which approximates reason—although we're not really privy to the salty dialogue the exorcist refers to. The pressure on the nuns is, naturally, intensified through any romantic (or even purely sexual) encounter with the opposite sex being virtually impossible for the members of the order. While Cutrara's description above provides a good general fit for most of the nuns seen in *The Devils*, he goes on to make an observation which seems tailor-made for Jeanne in particular:

> [The religious girl] is torn between her faith and reason. These cinematic struggles around sexual morality associate faith with a number of behaviors that are dangerous and irrational, running the gamut from fairly innocuous neuroses to those more severe, such as fanaticism and mental illness. (2014: 209)

Early on in the film, the Ursulines are seen desperately straining to catch a glimpse of the star of the show as Grandier leads the funeral procession for Saint-Marthe. It's Grandiermania, and has the air of, as Huxley puts it, the 'insane desire [...] of the schoolgirl for the crooner'—another example of a relatable, contemporary reference (1952: 107).[2] Jeanne subsequently tells Madeleine that a lack of dowries, not a love of God, is the chief reason for women entering the convent, and this information has a reductive effect, making it easy for the audience to view the nuns simply as sex-starved, repressed, immature women who don't need a second invitation to let rip when Father Barré requests a bawdy theatrical display. While Sister Jeanne may feel she's a class apart from these cavorting nuns—and no doubt considers her vengeful framing of Grandier to be an empowering move—in reality she's little more than a shill for the oppressive, patriarchal Church.

If heterosexuality and masculine/feminine roles are represented by Grandier and the various women he (mostly) walks across, this line of thinking is almost enlightened when compared to the film's representation of homosexuality. The first character we see in the film is King Louis XIII, clad in a clamshell bikini and leading a rococo-styled theatrical interpretation of Sandro Botticelli's painting *The Birth of Venus*. Androgynous in appearance, the king looks like a good and likely starting point for an exploration of what we now call gender fluidity, but sadly this does not develop; opening the film like this is quite the bold statement, and it's highly disappointing that a drag queen king rising in a half-shell marks the pinnacle of the film's examination of non-binary gender. Performing to a court which consists almost exclusively of bitchy transvestites (plus Cardinal Richelieu and a couple of accompanying nuns), the king's female attire, make-up and overripe theatricality seem to have been equated with his homosexuality: hardly progressive thinking.

King Louis' extravagant stage show.

This is a mere taste of what's to follow, however. When the king—camping it up in a large feathered hat and sparkly hose—visits the naked, hysterical nuns, he tells an accompanying boy that 'those are women, my darling. Look well. Vomit, if you wish.' Going on to describe women as 'gross things' and 'nasty', this version of Louis is not only homosexual and a cross dresser, but appears to be physically repulsed by women (the polar opposite of Grandier). It also seems we're meant to link the king's sexuality to his milk-and-water style of ruling the nation (and possibly even his casual cruelty); this Louis is little more than a puppet operated by Richelieu, and as long as the king gets to play dress-up and can shoot Protestants for sport (a complete fabrication which sees the film come within a whisker of jumping the shark), he doesn't seem to mind what happens to his country. On this evidence, the title 'Louis the Just' appears to be the ultimate misnomer. Russell's depiction of the royal family deferring to the Church—flagged as early as the pre-credits sequence in which Louis resentfully and nervously stoops to kiss the proffered hand of the Cardinal—seems somewhat at odds with Huxley's description: 'Politically powerful and strongly Gallican, the French monarchy had no reason to fear the Pope, and found the Church very useful as a machine for governing' (1952: 15). Although we might interpret Louis' lax approach as a sign that he's happy for the Church to do all the heavy lifting when it comes to running the country, the film paints the king as a figurehead under the Church's thumb, and he's reduced to little more than a cipher. If this is Gallicanism in action then it's certainly a very novel take on the concept, and one in which the tail is firmly wagging the dog; of course, the matter is muddied by the fact that Richelieu fulfilled a dual role, being both head of the Church in France and the country's first minister. Rumours abounded that Richelieu's successor, Mazarin, was the biological father of Louis XIV; while such gossip appeared to have no basis in fact, its mere existence nonetheless gave Louis XIII another good reason to be ill-disposed towards the Church.

With a gay presence on both sides of the camera during *The Devils*' production, it's rather surprising to see the heavy hand Russell uses when it comes to Louis. What makes it even more bizarre is that this portrayal is largely groundless. While the king's sexuality has long been debated, there appears to be no concrete evidence that this Bourbon monarch, father to the Sun King and the issue of Marie de' Medici and Henri IV, ever had a gay relationship; Huxley only goes as far as to state: 'In later life Louis XIII displayed a decided aversion for women, a decided, though probably platonic, inclination for men, and a decided repugnance for all kinds of physical deformity and disease' (1952: 19). In Russell's film, abhorrence replaces the softer-sounding aversion, and there is no reference to any phobia of malformation when Louis meets Jeanne while the bacchanalia rages in the church; the abbess even comes into close physical contact with the king, and their encounter concludes with Louis playfully rubbing Jeanne's chin and cheerfully telling her to 'have fun'.

Probably the furthest we can speculate is that Louis was a latent homosexual. With this in mind, it would be a different matter if Russell merely used the conjecture to drop a hint or two that the king may be something other than heterosexual, but to make Louis an openly gay man who hates women (yet loves wearing their clothes) is both historically inaccurate and needlessly tacky, and is one of the film's biggest, yet largely unnoted, transgressions. On the basis of the film, one would conclude that to be homosexual is to be effete and fey, just as to be heterosexual is to be either an alpha male or an omega female.

As Louis, the late Graham Armitage (somewhat bizarrely described by Russell as a 'leading transsexual' on the commentary for the BFI DVD) does terrifically well with what he's been given, but the part he's asked to interpret is as egregious and offensive as the role of I.Y.Yunioshi in *Breakfast at Tiffany's* (1961)—a monstrous Japanese caricature which has been widely, rightly pilloried. Both Louis and Yunioshi are hideous stereotypes, and in *The Devils*' case there was a further decade of significant progression to draw upon, which appears to have been steadfastly ignored when it came to this particular representation. It's almost as if Russell felt that his treatment of Tchaikovsky in *The Music Lovers* was a bit too subdued when it came to the composer's homosexuality (and subdued it wasn't), so this time around he'd make sure the point was hammered home. This is a seriously crass misstep in a film that's generally full of interesting ideas and questions, and lays Russell wide open to (unfortunately just) accusations of insensitivity. It's a depiction that does a real disservice to this otherwise deftly-handled film. While we do need to consider the time in which the film was made—homosexuality was frequently treated with disdain in the early 1970s (it had only been decriminalised in England and Wales in 1967)—Ken Russell was someone who clearly did know better. In terms of release dates, *The Devils* was virtually equidistant from *Performance* and *The Mother and the Whore*; if only Russell's film had exhibited a mere fraction of the sophisticated probing of sexual identity on display in those two works.

FOOTNOTES

1. When it comes to Sister Jeanne's language in the film, it seems likely that the censors inadvertently did Russell a big favour: Jeanne originally used the word 'cunt' at one stage (it was eventually redubbed as 'runt'), but the BBFC's John Trevelyan refused to permit it, citing the long battle he'd fought to get 'fuck' accepted. Russell vividly recalled Trevelyan saying: 'I'm afraid we can't have Vanessa [Redgrave] saying "cunt"' (Baxter, 1973, as cited in Crouse, 2012). As we know Jeanne isn't possessed, she seems an unlikely candidate to have such a word in

her vocabulary. Even when she, in an exchange with Father Mignon, uses the relatively tame 'cock', she giggles like a young child testing out a very naughty word. If Jeanne really was under a demonic influence, any and all profanity would be expected (cf. *The Exorcist*).

2. Russell would develop this idea more fully in *Lisztomania*, in which Franz Liszt, anachronistically presented as a rock star, can barely hear the music he's performing above the screams of the young girls who constitute his core audience. Most of the female characters in that film are defined by their relationships to Liszt who, like Grandier, is depicted as a serial womaniser.

Chapter 6: Versions and Censorship

The Devils is a film which, in the main, has not been well looked after since it debuted in cinemas in 1971. For the most part, the various versions of the film which exist are inextricably linked to its censorship history. The film has spent much of its life being squeezed on both sides, as both internal and external censorship have played their part in altering Russell's vision. This wasn't the first time a film had had its wings clipped by both Warner Bros. and the BBFC, as a similar fate had previously befallen *Performance* (Buck, 2012: 265–266). As Richard Crouse notes, trying to sort out the myriad versions of the film that are (or have been) available for home viewing is an almost impossible job (2012). Trying to compare various releases really is an onerous task, as running time—even when frame rate is taken into account—is no reliable guide, given that cuts can be made via substitution and transfers can happen at wonky speeds, plus there are the vagaries of distributor logos and so on. However, we can run through the film's main incarnations on the big screen, and also look at some of the home video options that are out there.

Loudun's walls are destroyed.

The original UK theatrical edition had a running time of 111 minutes, and remains the longest official version of the film currently available (although for many years this version was virtually impossible to see). The film caused problems at the BBFC, although secretary John Trevelyan and president Lord Harlech—thankfully, the two most influential members of the board—saw the sincerity in Russell's film and ensured it received a certificate (naturally, an X) with the minimum of cuts. Trevelyan was a fair, open-minded and thoughtful type who felt that extreme violence on screen could be justified if it helped illustrate a valid point, and this was very much his line of thinking as far as *The Devils* was concerned (Trevelyan, 1973: 162). However, a scene which neither the BBFC nor Warners felt should be included was the notorious 'Rape of Christ' sequence in which out-of-control nuns writhe naked on a life-sized crucifix, and we'll come to discuss this in a moment. Beyond this sequence being removed in its entirety, a further 132 feet (just under 90 seconds) of cuts were made before the film was deemed eligible for the BBFC stamp of approval. The censors and the studio sometimes, but not always, overlapped in their requests:

> Warners and the BBFC therefore drew up separate lists of the cuts they would require before the film could be distributed in the UK. In a number of cases the requirements of Warner Brothers and the BBFC coincided but a number of other cuts were unique to either Warners or the BBFC. Warners were content with the additional cuts requested by the BBFC, and vice versa, and a full list of required changes was forwarded to Russell. The cuts were intended to reduce (i) the explictness [sic] and duration of certain sexual elements, including an orgy of nuns, (ii) elements of violence and gore during an interrogation scene and the final burning, [...] and (iii) scenes that mixed sexual activity and religion in a potentially inflamatory [sic] fashion. ('The Devils', n.d.)

Ken Penry, a prominent member of the BBFC for nearly 20 years, had many misgivings about the film, which he described as 'nauseating' (contrasting with Trevelyan's assessment that it was 'brilliant'), and outlined what he felt would have to be changed if the film was to scrape through the classification process:

> [Penry] recommended the reduction of a scene where a nude woman plague victim is treated with leeches as well as the deletion of such shots in her pubic area; the considerable reduction of the fantasy scene in which Grandier descends from the cross to have his wounds licked by Sister Jeanne and then to make love to her; the drastic reduction of Sister Jeanne's syringe treatment, both anally and vaginally, and the removal of the word 'cunt'; the drastic reduction of all masturbation shots and the removal of nude women swinging on wheels; the drastic reduction of the scene

where pins are pushed through Grandier's tongue; the removal of the shots of Grandier's crushed legs after torture; the drastic reduction of the burning scene; and the elimination of the masturbation scene with Grandier's charred bone. (Robertson, 1989: 137)

Bringing out the dead: Grandier (centre) surveys plague victims.

That not all of these requests were actioned shows how the comparatively progressive Trevelyan was keen to shave off as little as possible from Russell's film, and censor and filmmaker were able to engage in a positive, productive and respectful running dialogue regarding what could stay and what must go. Although there were grumblings among other members of the board, Trevelyan helped steer the film through the process, and he was greatly aided by Harlech, a practising Catholic, who uncharacteristically blew a fuse when one dissenter questioned the sincerity of the work (Robertson, 1989: 138). By the time the film opened in the UK, Trevelyan had departed from his post and his successor, Stephen Murphy, was left to reap the storm. To his great credit, despite the decision to pass *The Devils* not happening on his watch, Murphy keenly defended both the film and the BBFC's decision, and made it clear that he felt Trevelyan had called this one correctly.

In the grand scheme of things, the fallout from *The Devils* was just another day at the office for Murphy, who within six months of his role commencing would have to deal with the inflammatory likes of *Straw Dogs* (1971) and *A Clockwork Orange*. Murphy's torrid tenure, which lasted just under four years (a long way short of the two decades Trevelyan worked for the board), coincided with a raft of other challenging titles including *Last House on the Left* (1972), *Heat* (1972), *The Exorcist*, *Last Tango in Paris* (1972), *Death Wish* (1974) and *Emmanuelle* (1974). More contentious material meant more censorship, and the following statistics help illuminate the board's activity during both the year and decade of *The Devils*: 1971 saw cuts made to just over 20% of films submitted, a high percentage which nonetheless was the joint *lowest* figure for the entire 1970s; the number of works censored peaked at nearly 34% in 1974, which is in sharp contrast to four decades on—2014 saw only 4.5% of films cut, and even that statistic is by far the highest to date for this century ('BBFC Statistics', n.d.). It's clear both the board and filmmakers now know how the game works, but the 70s saw such radical change in filmic content that a period of turbulence was inevitable. In addition to the impact it made in cinematic terms, *The Devils* stands as a key work in the history of film classification in the UK.

Receiving a certificate from the BBFC wasn't the end of *The Devils*' censorship problems on home soil, as UK local authorities reserve the right to overrule the BBFC's ratings for cinema releases—they can ban films that have been board-approved, screen films that haven't, and increase or decrease the level of the BBFC rating. In most cases, local councils don't bother with the extra workload and simply go along with BBFC certificates for films, sight unseen. In the event of controversial titles, however, local authorities will often take a look. Thus *The Devils* was banned by no less than 17 councils across the UK, including Cambridge and Glasgow—the latter of which also imposed a long-running embargo on another slice of religious controversy, *Life of Brian*. Even the progressive Greater London Council (GLC), which spent virtually all of its existence proudly out of step with the elected UK government and felt no pressing need to question the BBFC's work, was under pressure to ban both *The Devils* and *A Clockwork Orange* and took to the practice of reviewing selected titles (Wistrich, 1978: 21). Fortunately *The Devils* survived GLC inspection, and indeed its commercial prospects would have been severely damaged had the council decided to keep it off the capital's screens.

Many of *The Devils*' fans mourned the loss of the aforementioned 'Rape of Christ', feeling that the movie had had its heart ripped out—even though the sequence was never in the original release of the movie. Tellingly, Ken Russell himself said he felt the scene's reintroduction wouldn't alter the film in any significant way (Kermode, 1996). The

Moments before the fuse is lit, Father Barré taunts Grandier.

footage was considered lost until it turned up in 2002 following a search spearheaded by film critic Mark Kermode, and the film has since screened publicly with the restored footage in place. The brief scene at the end in which Jeanne masturbates with a bone was also added to this cut, and the quality of the 'new' footage, while not perfect, is pretty remarkable—you can clearly see that the 'Rape of Christ' sequence was a completely finished and processed one which was excised not long before the film's release, and it's amazing to consider how an outtake that no-one had been consciously looking after is so well-preserved. There's no great dip in quality, unlike with other recent examples of alternative versions of films with troubled histories such as *The Exorcist III* and *Once Upon A Time in America* (1984), where in both cases dreadful sub-VHS-level inserts have ironically made creatively compromised cuts seem far more attractive.

However, despite its good condition, the 'Rape of Christ' sequence is actually a fairly silly addition to *The Devils*, and one which both distracts and detracts from the rest of the film. Anyone who feels the sequence is the centrepiece of the film fails to recognise how the scene will be perceived by most who view it—and the relationship between art and those who consume it has to be a consideration when assessing any work. Such a sequence, had it remained, was always going to be the main talking point when discussing *The Devils*, and it would be a real pity if the rest of the film was eclipsed by this one scene. Perhaps it's a result of having seen the film far too many times without the sequence, but the 'Rape of Christ' is a jarring anomaly which does virtually nothing to propel the narrative; while Russell is making a point about how, in this situation, it's the Church that's affronting God, it's all but completely lost amidst the confrontational imagery. The same applies to Pier Paolo Pasolini's *Salo, or the 120 Days of Sodom* (1975)—most viewers who can endure the scenes in which victims are force-fed excrement are unlikely to immediately respond to it as the metaphor for consumerism Pasolini had in mind.

John Trevelyan felt the point had already been made in *The Devils'* orgy scene before the nuns descended on the crucifix, and he was quite right (ibid.). In addition, the sequence appears to have wandered in from another film, and its presence tips *The Devils* firmly into the realm of 'nunsploitation'—the rapid zooms in and out of Murray Melvin's Father Mignon, watching the events from on high while feverishly masturbating, really do belong in a 1970s B-movie, and the form of the scene is actually far more problematic than its content. While many may have fun with the likes of *Story of a Cloistered Nun* (1973), *The Devils* has far too much to say to risk being aligned with such fare; consider that even the 'Rape of Christ'-less theatrical edition was soon boiled down to a worryingly thin reduction of its more salacious moments—at least as far as the general public were concerned.

A graphic movie which contains a serious, sincere message will always struggle to convey its point, and the plight of such a film is not helped by extreme filmmaking which attempts to justify its content via spurious claims to analogy. A case in point is *A Serbian Film* (2010), one of the most relentlessly unpleasant films in recent years, which features no perceptible point yet its makers purport it to be a political allegory; it could be that an understanding of the film's message is dependent on an intricate knowledge of the history of the Republic of Serbia, but it's difficult to imagine anyone independently arriving at a conclusion matching the director's stated intentions. Calum Waddell made the incisive point that anyone who really desired to learn more about Serbia would be unlikely to seek out such a film as a resource (2010). Nonetheless, its tenuous allegorical status was deemed sufficient to secure a certificate from the BBFC (who were, we should remember, only classifying the film for the UK marketplace and its associated cultural reference points), although the board would only allow the film to be passed at 18 once around four minutes of cuts had been made.

But back to the 'Rape of Christ': the scene bears none of the classy look of the rest of the film as beautifully photographed by future Oscar winner David Watkin, and you could be forgiven for thinking that it was filmed by a rogue moonlighting crew à la Bob Guccione's inserts in *Caligula* (1979).[1] It's a wholly ridiculous sequence, one which, especially nowadays, seems far more likely to provoke hoots of derision than gasps of horror, and the film is much poorer for its inclusion. It is, nonetheless, a notable element of both the film's production and its censorship history—as such, it's a curio which would make for a very useful DVD bonus feature, and the successful effort to locate it should be applauded. The brief scene at the end of the film with Jeanne and Grandier's bone, on the other hand, works quite well, and while what Jeanne does with the 'souvenir' is obvious, it's only ever implied, and this restraint pays off as we are able to clearly sense the madness which has consumed the mother superior. The clarity of this scene contrasts with the over-egging nature of the 'Rape of Christ' sequence, and were Jeanne's final scene any more explicit it would completely obscure the intended message; sometimes, less really is more, even in a Ken Russell film. One small drawback is that the extended scene, regrettably, disrupts the neat match cut in which the femur landing on the convent floor meets Grandier's other bones and ashes being shovelled away.

The film's closing image: Madeleine leaves Loudun.

Although the original UK theatrical cut remains the best version of *The Devils*, things got much stickier when the film travelled across the Atlantic. Warners decided to go the route of pre-cutting the film themselves rather than enter into a dialogue with the

Motion Picture Association of America (MPAA), but the version submitted—shorn of not much short of three minutes, plus other cuts made via substitution—still landed the dreaded X certificate:

> While Trevelyan and Lord Harleck [sic] admired the version that finally became the British release cut, the U.S. was still breaking in its relatively new MPAA rating system and inevitably branded *The Devils* with an X, even after Warner Brothers cut additional gore and frontal nudity. In 1973, the studio wanted to cash in on the hubbub around *The Exorcist* and sliced more off for an R. Sadly, this would be the version, with a noisome pan-and-scan transfer and terrible sound, that the studio finally released on home video in 1981 and for which Great Britain would also have to settle. (Lanza, 2007)

The version which secured an R in 1973 was only slightly modified from the previous US cut. The film—apparently commercially dead as far as Warners were concerned—was then, as Joseph Lanza notes above, ignominiously used as a barker to attract customers to *The Exorcist*, which, as already established, was fare that Warners considered to be far more acceptable. As Lanza also points out, this truncated cut became the main edition in circulation on video in the US, UK, or anywhere else, if indeed it could be tracked down at all—and as it turns out, if you can remember back to the introduction, there really was a UK VHS of the film floating around in the early 1980s. This edition, boxed in the highly collectable clamshell case Warners used for at least some of their rental titles, occasionally turns up for sale online. But getting back to the theatrical editions: there is a further twist in that the Internet Movie Database (IMDb) notes that a UK version exists with around 10 minutes chopped out, seemingly for temporal reasons—this cut would be short enough to form part of double bill, and could therefore enjoy a run on the repertory circuit. This could well be the one I saw in the 1980s. Besides it forming one half of a double feature (with *Jubilee*), what leads me to this conclusion is that I distinctly, unashamedly remember the scene in which Sister Agnes (or Sister Judith, if you prefer to go by the credits) masturbates the church candle, the presence of which indicates this version was cut for length not content (the longer UK cut had a certificate anyway, so a trimmed down edition of this version would almost certainly incur no censorial problems). This shot was excised from the US cut, which discounts that as being the version which screened, but of course I, like the esteemed critic Alexander Walker, am not beyond pareidolia as far as *The Devils* is concerned.[2]

It wasn't until the early 1990s that the film became available on sell-through video in the UK—while BBFC records show Warners as having submitted the film as early as January 1988, I don't recall it appearing on shelves and being marketed until mid-1990, when it was issued as one of five Russell films under the banner 'Masters of the Movies' (Warners didn't appear to think such a group included Russell when the film was first released).[3] Such a delay isn't impossible, but is rather unusual, and of course this edition—rated 18 with no BBFC cuts imposed—contained the US version. This marked the first time the film had been submitted to the BBFC for a home video certificate. In August 1997 Warners did surprise everyone, however, in submitting the UK theatrical cut to the BBFC, which was passed uncut at 18, and was promptly released as part of a VHS series which also included the likes of *Performance*, *Blade Runner* (1982), *The Right Stuff* (1983) and *The Man Who Fell to Earth* (1976). This collection came under the collective banner of 'Maverick Directors' (read: films which initially flopped and/or caused problems for the distributor, who subsequently realised a quick buck could be made by marketing them as cult fare). This fine quality (for VHS, anyway) edition marked serious progress, and in terms of official home video releases this cut remains the longest available, with any subsequent upgrades only improving on the sound and picture quality. But it is rather strange to think that this release, on antiquated videotape, has not been extended upon as far as official home viewing is concerned.

Of course, the film's life on the big screen is another matter, and within five years of the 'Maverick Directors' VHS edition the aforementioned 'Rape of Christ' footage had been recovered and, along with Jeanne's bone scene, subsequently re-inserted into the film for a 2004 screening at London's National Film Theatre (NFT). The footage had been seen prior to this in *Hell On Earth* (2002), a documentary on the film which aired on UK station Channel 4. This restoration has enjoyed a few more outings on the big screen beyond its initial NFT appearance, but has never been given an official DVD release.

Both *Hell On Earth* and the 2004 restoration led to renewed interest in the film, and it wasn't long before a couple of bootleg DVDs appeared which incorporated the 'Rape of Christ' into the film proper. The quality of these discs was not great, although they did provide a fine opportunity for the many fans who couldn't get along to any of the few theatrical screenings to see an approximation of the restored version. They also remain the only physical home video versions available which incorporate the 'Rape of Christ' footage. Some useful insights into the origin and background of these bootleg editions were provided by 'Wanyon', a user on an internet forum. Wanyon explains how he/she created a composite cut using the 'Maverick Directors' VHS as a base print and inserted the 'Rape of Christ' scene from *Hell on Earth*; they also mention how they had hoped to include the bone scene, but a voiceover precluded them from doing so, although later on they realised that a small adjustment to the SCART cable would have made this possible (2010).

The first official DVD of *The Devils* appeared in Spain in 2010, and although it was the US cut of the film, it was a fine-looking disc (it was taken from a theatrical print), and was a must for all who'd waited for a decent home video version. This edition, as well as missing everything you'd expect the US cut to leave out, contains an additional, baffling alteration in that Richelieu's early line 'and may the Protestant be driven from the land' has been cut, apparently by someone with a blindfold and a very rusty pair of scissors; Richelieu gets as far as opening his mouth to deliver the line before being rudely shut down as we cut to a skull with maggots dripping from its mouth (at least it makes for an amusing match cut, of sorts). Quite why this line, which immediately and importantly marks out the Cardinal's hatred of Huguenots, was removed is anyone's guess—it could possibly be a product of the censorship of Franco-era Spain, but one would have thought that the General would have endorsed the sentiments expressed by Richelieu. This edition appears to be the basis for a Korean DVD edition of questionable legality, as everything about the Korean disc is identical to the Spanish release, with the exception of the artwork and the addition of Korean subtitles.[4]

Another Spanish DVD release appeared in 2016, this time containing the original UK theatrical version. Between the two Spanish releases, however, came the BFI DVD. This 2012 two-disc release is an edition which many have mixed feelings about—while both sound and picture quality are excellent, it's still the original UK theatrical version of the film, with no additional material added, and the 'Rape of Christ' sequence isn't even to be found anywhere among the extras (*Hell On Earth* is present on the second disc, but with the scene now removed—although some substitute footage brings the running time up to that of the original TV broadcast). Barring the briefest of snippets, Warners would not allow the 'Rape of Christ' footage to be included anywhere on this release, nor would they hand over the materials needed for a Blu-ray edition (Warners supplied the film on DigiBeta, a format which does push the upper limits of standard definition [SD], but it still comes over as a passive-aggressive move). The film does look especially great considering it isn't on a high definition (HD) disc, and there are plentiful extras; but there's a frustration in the best quality release we have of the film being a version we've had no trouble seeing since 1997, and on a format which was becoming outdated even back in 2012. Although my own preference for the film is the UK theatrical cut, I would have welcomed the inclusion of the 2004 restoration on the disc, with seamless branching providing the viewer with the choice of two different versions, but the lack of such an option is something which remains beyond the BFI's control. That Russell happily approved this edition (although, sadly, he died just a few months before its release) shows that this is no bastardised version, and it certainly shouldn't be considered to have been cut in the conventional sense. With Warners' refusal to hand over any more footage or an HD master, this does look like it will be as good as it gets for The Devils on home video.

And just as home video provides more options than the cinema, the internet gives yet more possibilities to view the film in a version of your liking. The film turned up in the US iTunes store in 2010, before being pulled a few days later without any explanation (a US DVD of the UK theatrical cut was announced for 2008, but never materialised). The film has since reappeared on iTunes and now seems here to stay on both the US and UK sites, and while it is the US cut of the film on both sides of the Atlantic, it does look and sound very good and on technical merit is probably a better option than the first Spanish DVD.

With *Hell On Earth* being made and broadcast during the internet age, it was only ever going to be a matter of time before someone imported some of its material into an official version of the film and shared the quite unofficial results online. Wanyon's edit mentioned earlier originated from an altruistic, enthusiastic fan with a VHS deck and a DVD recorder, before this non-profit venture fell into the hands of opportunistic types who sold a compressed version of it, very much for profit, on many sites including some high-profile e-tailers. One of the labels which co-opted this labour of love betrayed their lack of knowledge of the content by prominently crediting 'Venessa' Redgrave and Ken 'Russel' on the front cover.

Fanedits of films now enjoy great popularity online, with a number of sites seriously devoted to the non-profit pursuit of creating improved, or at least different, versions of existing films. George Lucas' *Star Wars* (1977) and its first two sequels have been painstakingly 'despecialised' to get them into shape as high-quality editions of the original theatrical releases, and Lucas' fellow movie brat Brian De Palma liked the fanedit of his *Raising Cain* (1992) so much that he requested it be included on the Blu-ray release. So it perhaps comes as no surprise that someone has taken the excellent starting point of the BFI DVD of *The Devils* and has added in both the 'Rape of Christ' sequence and the bone scene, with the latter requiring some deft work on the sound to replace Vanessa Redgrave's voiceover from *Hell on Earth* with a piece of music. This version of the film is very impressive, and the editor has even gone to the trouble of removing the banner that flashed up on screen during the 'Rape of Christ' scene in the *Hell on Earth* broadcast. Although obviously not an official release, this version will at least have been seen by far more people than have ever managed to catch the 2004 restoration on a cinema screen, and many of the film's biggest followers will no doubt have found a way to track down this fanedit. While this release, after a fashion, fulfils the wishes of many who'd like to see the film with the 2002 footage inserted, it still wasn't in HD.

However, following this composite cut, a version appeared online that seemed to be basically the same, but *was* in high definition. Unlike the previously discussed fanedit, the source for this release has not been confirmed, but many think it's likely to have been taken from a TV broadcast. The numbers do check out (as in, it is an HD file), but regardless of the source this is a fantastic-looking version, and its (admittedly limited) presence goes some way towards filling the gap created by Warners' refusal to sanction anything beyond the SD theatrical cut. While Warners have been criticised far and wide for their handling of *The Devils*, we should remember that they are in no way obliged to license the film to anyone. And it is possible, though highly unlikely, that the reason for blocking an HD version is that Warners may consider doing such a release themselves one day and weren't keen on handing over the Blu-ray rights. This possibility does seem remote, however, as the film isn't even available on DVD in the US. But there is something paradoxical about Warners' treatment of the film—if they wanted to bury the film they could do just that, but it's almost as if they can't quite make up their minds as to what they should do with it, and are therefore keeping it alive in a limited, carefully managed fashion. Every legal available version exists solely because of Warners' say-so, and if they really feel so strongly about the film being out there they actually have no pressing need for its entire revenue stream, much less the BFI's widow's mite.

So, in terms of legally owning the film, what should you do? There are obviously very limited options, and it basically comes down to a straight choice between the BFI disc (running time: c. 107 minutes) for those who prefer physical media and copious extras (and have a player that handles Region 2 DVDs), while those who favour digital downloads (or can't play Region 2 discs) should grab the iTunes release (running time: c. 108 minutes).[5] While the BFI disc obviously has the longer cut and is the best legal version in any format, it should be said that *The Devils*' burning brilliance shines through in any of the versions discussed here—while Ken Russell, quite understandably, considered the butchered US cut to be a complete waste of time, it nonetheless does stand up fairly well. It's all rather ironic that the film garnered its current level of interest partly because of a sequence that we now can't officially see (at least not in the context of the film). The film's censorship problems were huge from the very beginning, but it seems that, over 45 years on from its initial release, the main barrier to seeing the longest possible version of the film is the studio that owns it.

Father Mignon begins to doubt Grandier's guilt.

The Devils' censorship problems make for an interesting comparison when we consider the controversy whipped up by a much more recent title, *The Passion of the Christ* (2004). While members of churches and other religious organisations turned out in droves to see the movie—contributing to the film becoming the highest-grossing R-rated film of all time—the film was the source of some very heated debate, with accusations of historical/biblical inaccuracy and anti-Semitism being levelled at this very singular vision of Christ's torturous death. Nathan Rabin referred to it as a 'grindhouse take on the crucifixion' (2010: 97). *The Hollywood Reporter* commented on the film's 'near pornographic violence' (Honeycutt, 2004, as cited in Godawa, 2009: 193). David Denby, in his review in *The New Yorker*, went as far as to call the film a 'sickening death trip, a grimly unilluminating procession of treachery, beatings, blood and agony' (2004). It's unusual for such a controversial, extreme, violent and gory title to become a bona fide blockbuster, but with such a huge readymade Christian audience awaiting the film, box-office respectability was almost guaranteed, even if it did become profitable way beyond the wildest of predictions. Both the film and its equally militant army of supporters were so convinced they were on the side of good, that in the end any dissenting voices were all but drowned out. Much like the reverse of what happened with *The Devils*, really. *The Passion*'s perceived moralism reeled in the type of audience who gave Russell's film the slip, on account of its adjudged blasphemy. The two films do have something in common, beyond stirring up religious controversy, in that both saw an inordinate amount of pre-release discussion as their level of suitability was ascertained. The scholars and activists who harboured concerns regarding the production of *The Passion* were quick to take on the challenge:

> They judged the film to be in violation of academic consensus [...] of post-Vatican II guidelines governing Catholic presentation of Jews and Judaism in preaching, teaching and dramatisation. These interventions proved largely ineffectual [...] — in part because they demonstrated little insight into the specific challenges facing those who try to film the life and death of Jesus. In a telling illustration of this gap in understanding, the most vociferous scholars based their initial arguments on their reading of the screenplay, whilst [director Mel] Gibson's canny and successful response was to organise screenings that allowed people to see a rough version of the film. (Wright, 2007: 25)

Again, this plays out rather like an inversion of *The Devils*' censorship situation, in which Russell's script had been seen by the studio and was cut simply as it was considered to be too long, only for vehement objections to be raised once the words on the page had come to life and the film screened to both Warners and the BBFC. *The Devils*' editor Michael Bradsell recalls how the studio accused Russell of not making the film as per the script, and maintains that such charges were completely unfounded (Crouse, 2012). Russell may have acted with admirable transparency in making his script available to view, but we all know how the image dwarfs the word, and that's assuming that the screenplay was subjected to particularly thorough inspection in the first place (United Artists, the backers of Russell's previous three feature films and initial financiers for *The Devils*, got cold feet when they eventually got around to studying the script). While Gibson's film faced no real censorship problems when it came to getting his film classified (it was passed as R in the US and 18 in the UK; in 1971 it would have struggled to receive any certificate at all), the director did apply a form of self-censorship when he subsequently produced a re-edited version which toned down the near-constant brutality (and *Godsmacked*, an impish fanedit of the film, sees close to an hour removed and a set of new, completely inaccurate subtitles added). Shorn of a good portion of what Manohla Dargis referred to as 'ecstatic, almost sexualized' violence, Gibson's 15 (UK)/unrated (US) cut of the film, while still a punishing experience, actually plays far better than the original edit (2005). However, this truncated release met with little interest and soon limped out of cinemas, which may tell us something of the bloodlust of those who'd stampeded to catch the unexpurgated version.

Jesus is mocked and beaten by Roman soldiers in The Passion of the Christ.

Upon seeing *The Passion* on its initial release, I was impressed with its technical accomplishments and the steadfastly anti-commercial decision to film in Aramaic and Latin (Gibson would have to relent on his wish for the film to screen *sans* subtitles, though—and an English dub would eventually surface in 2017), but the more I reflected on it the more I realised that there is a conspicuous absence of spirituality amidst the blood and violence… actually, there is no 'amidst' the blood and violence, as Gibson's film is so one-paced that there is absolutely no breathing room for a sense of spirituality to emerge. The film is so obsessed with detailing the physical agony of Christ's death that it effectively sidelines his teachings (Rabin, 2010: 29). The more I've thought about the film (I've seen both the 18 and 15-rated versions), the more pointlessly horrifying it becomes, and the suffocating evil on display, coupled with the lack of any tonal shifts, makes it impossible to see from where anything enlightening could possibly emerge.

As crushing as the none-too-pious Grandier's death is in *The Devils*, there is some hope in the film as we witness the firm conviction which sees Grandier burn rather than deny his faith. *The Passion*, on the other hand, is little more than an X-rated spin on a story most already know; it's the *Via Crucis* come to life—but do we really need it to leap from church walls and into glorious Technicolor? Must we endure the elided material? Even the ending of *The Passion* (which lines up with the 14th and final Station of the Cross), which sees Christ resurrected, cannot take the edge off the numbness one feels after sitting through two almost invariably brutal hours which utterly fail to provide any spiritual nourishment. Like *The Passion*, *The Devils* is not an uplifting experience, but unlike Gibson's effort Ken Russell's film is imbued with a sincerity, and does feature moments when we can get a very real and clear sense of a man's faith becoming stronger and deeper even as his life spins out of control. It is by no means inapt to consider that *The Devils* 'may be one of the most honest, progressive documents of what true faith and Godliness represents' (Alexander, 2017). While it might seem remarkable to many to suggest that *The Devils* is a more edifying work than *The Passion of the Christ*, Russell's probing and questioning film works with the viewer in order to come up with a sense of right and wrong; more crucially, it refrains from dogma.

The Gospel According to St. Matthew (1964), another film by Pier Paolo Pasolini—a director who, much like Ken Russell, was also lazily caricatured by the tabloid press as an *enfant terrible*—is another unlikely source of spirituality, or at least its Marxist director is. Pasolini was able to make a nuanced, moving and stimulating version of Christ's story, but, as with Russell, the director's reputation is enough for many to discount exploring the film. That so many more people turned out to watch *The Passion of the Christ* than queued up for either *The Devils* or *The Gospel According to St. Matthew* suggests that audiences are looking in the wrong places for films which contain serious moral and spiritual elements. Although both Russell and Pasolini already had rather outré public personas when they made their films—which almost certainly led to audiences approaching their works with prejudice—*The Passion of the Christ*'s director Mel Gibson would see his own public image turn very sour within a couple of years of his film's release, long after its huge commercial success had been attained.[6] Both Gibson and Russell were practising Catholics when they made their films, but Pasolini felt it was only his atheism which made it possible for him to film the story (Greene, 1990: 122). Of the three films, Pasolini's is by far the least graphic (it was awarded a U certificate by the BBFC), and it is perhaps worth considering how the detachment (of sorts) Pasolini felt towards his subject resulted in a work which was entirely free from confrontational imagery.

The unusual and one-off nature of *The Passion of the Christ* can make it a fairly difficult film to judge, but if we take it at face value (and we really should), a fair assessment of its content can be found in the BBFC's take on *Grotesque* (2009)—a title which was refused a UK certificate—which board director David Cooke described as 'featur[ing] minimal narrative or character development and present[ing] the audience with little more than an unrelenting and escalating scenario of humiliation, brutality and sadism' ('BBFC Rejects', 2009). *Grotesque*, for all its stomach-churning violence, is at least a much more honest endeavour than the rebarbative, aforementioned *A Serbian Film* in that it never pretends to be anything other than a flat-out gorefest. Perhaps if the makers of *Grotesque*, who cheerfully took BBFC rejection on the chin, had claimed their film was analogous, then it may have scraped past the board, albeit with some cuts. Any point in *The Passion of the Christ* is befogged by its graphic content in a way which makes Russell's message in *The Devils* seem obvious in comparison. In any case, it is doubtful that the BBFC's oft-cited yardstick, the man on the Clapham omnibus, could extract a moral from either *Grotesque* or *The Passion of the Christ* when faced with such blood, noise and chaos. That *Grotesque* was rejected by the BBFC and *The Passion* sailed through uncut firmly demonstrates that perceived intent is often the deal-breaker when extreme content is encountered, and John Trevelyan and Lord Harlech did well to look beyond *The Devils*' sensational surface, even when acutely aware that the majority of the film-going public would not.

FOOTNOTES

1. David Watkin won an Oscar for his work on *Out of Africa* (1985). Just a few years after *The Devils*, he would again film Oliver Reed in both *The Three Musketeers* (1973) and *The Four Musketeers* (1974)—two films which, in Cardinal Richelieu and Louis XIII, shared characters with *The Devils*.
2. Walker, in an infamous televised exchange with Ken Russell (which culminated in the director swearing and whacking the critic with a rolled-up newspaper), claimed that the film included a shot of Grandier's crushed genitals—which, in any version, it most definitely didn't (Crouse, 2012).
3. The other four titles in the series were *Women in Love*, *The Music Lovers*, *Lisztomania* and *Valentino* (1977).
4. The copy of the Korean disc I watched had a problem in that the original audio track was slightly yet noticeably out of sync with the picture. Whether this was just a single defective copy or the fault ran to other (or all) discs in the print run is impossible to say, as this was the only copy of this edition I viewed.
5. Don't be fooled into thinking that the iTunes release is more complete than the BFI DVD—while it may be slightly longer on the face of it, this is simply due to the differing frame rates of the two versions. If the iTunes version played at the same frame rate as the BFI disc, it would only run to c. 103 minutes. Similarly, frame rate differences mean that the running time of the BFI disc is less than that of the original UK cinema release—but the actual content is identical.
6. Mel Gibson was at the centre of a well-publicised incident in 2006, when he was arrested for driving under the influence of alcohol and responded with an anti-Semitic rant.

Chapter 7: Legacy

As time progresses and we get further away from 1971 and the period in which *The Devils* first appeared, the unique nature of the film becomes ever more apparent. As previously discussed, there is virtually no way in which it can be considered a time capsule of its era, as the film's content is atypical for the early 1970s and its message is an enduring one. It also sidesteps categorisation in a way which prevents it being lumped in with certain types of films of the time—exploitation, sexploitation, nunsploitation, and so on, although many of the movie's harsher critics would be more than happy to attach at least one of those reductive labels to Russell's film; conversely, Ian Olney, while recognising *The Devils*' merits and achievements, sees the film as a key synergist in nunsploitation (2013: 175). As *The Devils* was backed by Warner Bros., for all of the continuing problems between the studio and the film, the association with a company not aligned with a particular genre has arguably been a saving grace. This has precluded the film from being thought of as part of a run of post-war UK horror where, for the most part, studio branding overrode the individual merits and identities of films—the most obvious example of this being with the films of Hammer, but also including (to a lesser extent) those of both Amicus and Tigon. Between them, these three production companies made some fine films and also some very poor ones, but the quality of the individual titles has been rendered largely irrelevant as the received wisdom is that any film by any one of these studios is interchangeable with the next. Unfair as that perception may be, such fare has been ring-fenced as part of a fad specific to a period, and Russell's film is lucky in that an accident of financial backing has allowed it to live on free from such negative associations. Had *The Devils* been made under such a studio, Tigon would doubtless have made for the most accommodating backers, seeing as they seemed to have a bit more ambition in making historical drama with a real edge—as evidenced by both *Witchfinder General* and *The Blood on Satan's Claw*.

A similar fate was famously in store for Robin Hardy's *The Wicker Man* (1973), another film made outside of those three very recognisable UK horror studios. As with *The Devils*, *The Wicker Man* was backed by a company (British Lion) whose name didn't eclipse the film, and Hardy's movie was also subjected to studio interference as it was pushed and pulled around, eventually appearing in several different versions of varying lengths. At one stage, Warner Bros. were involved in the US distribution of the film, and, as seems may well have been the case with *The Devils*, *The Wicker Man* was hacked back in order to play as part of a double bill (it would serve as supporting feature to another British Lion film, Nicolas Roeg's excellent *Don't Look Now* [1973]). Further parallels with *The Devils* can be made in that there was a search for missing footage from *The Wicker Man*, which was similarly successful but differed in its final outcome in that the found material was officially released (unlike Warners with *The Devils*, rights holders Canal+ were keen for *The Wicker Man* to be seen in as complete a version as possible). *The Wicker Man*, in any of its incarnations, is an intriguing and unsettling film yet one whose power arguably diminishes with every passing year. While it may have dodged a bullet in being financed by a backer not synonymous with horror (although the presence of horror—and Hammer—icon Christopher Lee comes close to neutralising that status) and is to be lauded for its avoidance of gore and cheap scares, it now looks aesthetically dated in a way which makes it too easy for audiences to laugh at, which unfortunately undermines and dilutes the spell cast by Hardy and writer Anthony Shaffer. It may take place on a remote island, but the film is all too connected to the familiar, and the firmly recognisable twentieth-century milieu has, over time, proved to be the undoing of *The Wicker Man*. Conversely, *The Devils* occurs in a time that no viewer ever lived through and thus manages to avoid such pitfalls. While the cult of *The Wicker Man* endures (in spite of Hardy's poor, belated sequel *The Wicker Tree* [2011]), the film is too obviously of its time to be wholly effective in the present day. While it diverges from *The Devils* in this key sense, it is nonetheless a film which may be the closest we have to a comparison for Russell's film—at least in terms of it being another 1970s film which operated outside of the norm for UK horror, and one which endured a similarly rocky release history which resulted in multiple versions in circulation.

But this only goes to prove just how difficult it is to come up with correlations with Russell's film. *The Devils* is sometimes referred to as influential, but it's hard to trace a line back to it from most films you might care to think of. As mentioned in chapter 3, some of the imagery in *The Exorcist* does appear to have riffed on *The Devils*, but of course the novel it was based on was published just before Russell's film debuted in cinemas, which gives the film a convenient source in which to cite all of its inspiration. But finding films since *The Devils* that are like *The Devils* is very difficult—at best, there are a handful of films which appropriate its mood in places: The *Name of the Rose* (1986), despite being set around 300 years earlier, successfully mixes Catholicism, sensuality, politics and perceived heretics against the backdrop of a murder mystery; Peter Greenaway's *The Baby of Mâcon* (1993)—arguably the most extreme entry in its director's filmography—sees a vindictive Church order a multiple rape and execution of someone who's got in its way; *Elizabeth* (1998) memorably portrays the Church as an imposing, intransigent and terrifying entity; *The Reckoning* (2002), while falling way short of its excellent source novel *Morality Play*, follows a wayward priest who's had a sexual relationship with a member of his parish; and Luc Besson's underrated *The Messenger* (1999), while not many people's Joan of Arc film of choice, makes a fine job of showing how someone with a firm and sincere relationship with God perishes at the stake.

While each of these films, as described, contain aspects of plot or action which, however prominent, are recognisable from *The Devils*—and it would be fairly easy to find more examples of such movies—what's more notable is that they all, to varying extents, possess a specific pervading tone which recalls Russell's film. The Church figures to some degree in each of these films, and most of the stories feature victimisation, but the most notable aspect shared by all is a keen sense of oppression associated with the Church and the sorry fates of those who, despite remaining largely on the side of good, fail to fall in line with the institution. The supernatural does not figure, at least not significantly, in any of these films, which leaves them to draw on other sources for their unsettling effect, and, just as in *The Devils*, each work taps into the idea that a horror which may seem to be a product of the magical or paranormal actually has its origins in man—what Leibniz termed metaphysical evil. While *The Devils* was not the first film to posit this, it is perhaps the most effective screen illustration of the concept and as such has influenced works including those mentioned above. Of those five films, the one which most overtly betrays the influence of *The Devils* is actually Shekhar Kapur's *Elizabeth*, a historical drama with real bite which, despite depicting events which occurred decades before those in Russell's film, could almost be seen to begin where *The Devils* ends:

> [T]he film [...] begins with a graphic depiction of the burning at the stake of three 'Protestant heretics' in post-Reformation England. A woman and two men are roughly shaved, bound, and then led toward the stake. Several overhead shots give viewers a sense of looking down on the violent proceedings. The crowd surges forward,

though soldiers keep them back. The flames begin to lick up towards the victims. A darkly robed, bearded, official reads out the following in gruff tones: 'By order of their gracious majesties Queen Mary and Prince Philip we have come to witness the burning of these Protestant heretics who have denied the authority of the one true Catholic Church and His Holiness the Pope. Let them burn for all eternity in the flames of Hell.' (Mitchell, 2014: 285)

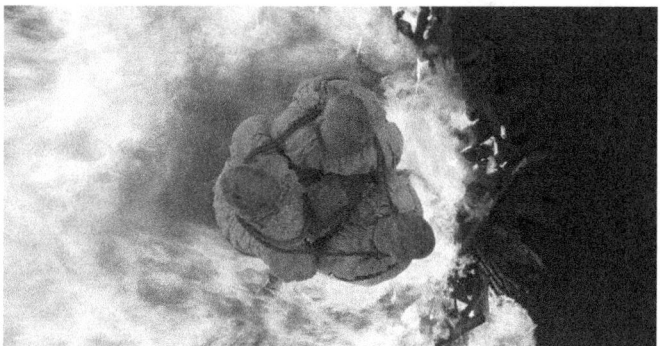

Protestants burn in Shekhar Kapur's Elizabeth.

While such a description sounds extremely familiar to those conversant with *The Devils*—and provides yet more grim evidence that such practices predate Urbain Grandier's death (and birth)—*Elizabeth* is very much its own film, and is a highly effective post-*Devils* work in its portrayal of how man's cruelty quickly outstrips that of any supposed evil spirit. While *Elizabeth* and *The Devils* do sometimes converge in a very broad sense, there are odd details in Kapur's film which will resonate with those who know Russell's film back to front, such as when, roughly two minutes into the film (just before the burning described above), there's an aerial shot of a priest's cross-emblazoned gloves which vividly recalls the attire of Father Barré; this does seem more homage than coincidence.

Like Russell, Kapur does not let recorded history get in the way of getting his message across, as the two men (Nicholas Ridley, Hugh Latimer) who in reality were burned at the stake are joined in the film by a third, fictional, female victim (ibid.). It may be tempting to dismiss *Elizabeth* as just another Oscar-baiting costume drama, but the choice of a director like Shekhar Kapur—hitherto best known for the controversial

Bandit Queen (1994)—signals that this project is striving for something a bit beyond the typically lush historical drama that somewhat characterised this period of British cinema. While the movie is sufficiently orthodox so as not to give production company Working Title any real cause for concern, Kapur manages to imbue proceedings with enough in the way of off-kilter touches to engage those normally averse to films of this ilk. With its major plotline of Catholics vs. Protestants, there is plenty here for fans of *The Devils*, but unlike *La Reine Margot*, Kapur's film does take on the Church, and the results are not especially sympathetic. At around the film's halfway point, Elizabeth proposes the Act of Uniformity and is roundly shouted down by the bishops and other clergymen— the disrespect on display seems to be due to Elizabeth being a woman as opposed to what she's saying. As the nervous queen makes her way in to state her case, there's a disquieting point of view shot of the bishops towering over Elizabeth, grimly staring down at the ruler as they reluctantly move aside. This shot is rather terrifying in itself, but also symbolises a hierarchy—official or otherwise—as essayed in *The Devils*, in which the Church deems itself superior to both monarchy and State. The patriarchal nature of the Church and how women are viewed within it is underlined by this shot in particular and the scene in general—you really cannot imagine the clergymen rounding on a male monarch in this fashion.

Stern bishops receive the title character in Elizabeth.

Kapur does manage to shoehorn a sliver of Russell's sentiments as witnessed in *The Devils* into *Elizabeth*, and the two directors are certainly partial to revisionism as they make their points via historical events. *Elizabeth* was a great critical and commercial success and attracted no controversy—unlike its pale, lacklustre sequel *Elizabeth: The Golden Age* (2007), which saw Kapur accused of both anti-Catholicism and wild historical inaccuracy.

It is worth considering how the film affected Ken Russell's subsequent forays and where *The Devils* ranks in his entire body of work. With *The Devils*' follow-up taking the form of musical Twiggy vehicle *The Boy Friend* (which featured a good sprinkling of *The Devils*' supporting cast), and the film after *The Boy Friend* being the low-key artist biopic *Savage Messiah* (1972), it does appear that there was a conscious pulling away by the director from the intense ferocity of *The Devils*. The wholesome family affair of *The Boy Friend* looks very much like an antidote for *The Devils*, although it didn't appear to be much fun for Russell, who again had to deal with studio interference when around 25 minutes were removed for the film's US release. While Russell's output for the rest of his career should certainly not be dismissed—although it frequently is—it's safe to say none of his films subsequent to *The Devils* managed to better it. However, it may just be that one or two of his films prior to 1971 are equal to *The Devils*—both *Women in Love* and the made-for-TV Delius biopic *Song of Summer* (1968) are exceptionally well-crafted efforts which display an evenness and sureness of touch which isn't evident in much of Russell's post-*Devils* work.

Russell would go on to make other films which pushed at the boundaries of censorship—*Crimes of Passion* being a particular case in point—and with his trio of movies for Vestron would film adaptations of works by noted writers Oscar Wilde, Bram Stoker, and, in a move which smacked of going back to the well, D. H. Lawrence, but nothing ever emerged which could come close to matching the lightning-in-a-bottle moment that was *The Devils*. After the way in which the stars aligned for Russell's Huxley-Whiting adaptation, which was a career highlight for many involved, it seemed that Russell, broadly speaking, had two main modes of operation: one where he'd try a bit too hard (*The Boy Friend*, *Valentino*), the other where he'd lazily lapse into being cartoonishly offensive and would send himself up (*Lizstomania*, *The Lair of the White Worm*). Frequently, as with *Altered States*—something of a bellwether for his career from then on—these two modes would run in parallel.

Over the course of this book I have tried to explain the importance of *The Devils* both to and beyond the horror genre. As evidenced here, it is a film which concurrently exists both within and without of horror, which may preclude it from the type of analysis one might typically apply to works in the genre. The presence of a timeless, universal message should not be seen as a sign that Ken Russell is merely using the genre as a vehicle on which to relay loftier concerns, but rather proof that some of the best horror films have an exceptionally long reach. It is not so much a film which works on different levels, but rather one in which the political and the personal, the fine detail and the broad canvas, the earth-shattering and the life-changing all collude and shift around in the same space, ready mixed for viewer consumption. The audience does not have to process the film in terms of layers, or separate the literal from the analogous, as with *The Devils* Ken Russell created a work which affords the viewer that rarest of opportunities: to simultaneously think and feel.

BIBLIOGRAPHY

Alexander, Chris. 'Ken Russell's The Devils Premieres on Shudder.' *Comingsoon.net*. AtomicOnline, 15 Mar. 2017. Web. 23 Nov. 2017. <http://www.comingsoon.net/horror/features/826071-ken-russells-the-devils-premieres-on-shudder>.

Bazin, André, *What is Cinema?* (Hugh Gray, Trans.), Berkeley: University of California Press, 1967.

'BBFC Rejects Sexually Violent Japanese Horror DVD.' *British Board of Film Classification*. BBFC, 19 Aug. 2009. Web. 20 June 2017. <http://www.bbfc.co.uk/about-bbfc/media-centre/bbfc-rejects-sexually-violent-japanese-horror-dvd>.

'BBFC Statistics.' *British Board of Film Classification*. BBFC, n.d. Web. 16 October 2017. <http://www.bbfc.co.uk/website/statistics.nsf >.

Billington, Michael, *State of the Nation: British Theatre Since 1945*, London: Faber, 2007.

Black, Andy, *Oliver Reed: Ten Top Movies*, London: Creation Books, 1999.

Black, Conrad, *Duplessis*, Toronto: McClelland and Stewart, 1977.

Blatty, William Peter, *The Exorcist: 40th Anniversary Edition*, New York: HarperCollins, 2011.

'Booming number of exorcisms in France.' *Connexion* July &Aug. 2017: 3. Print.

Bourne, Thomas. 'The Devils.' *The History Web*. University of St. Andrews, n.d. Web. 27 Apr. 2017. <https://www.st-andrews.ac.uk/~histweb/scothist/brown_k/film/closed/reviews/devils.html>.

Bridle, Marc. 'World Premiere: The Devils (uncut version).' *Film Music on the Web*. MusicWeb International, Dec. 2004. Web. 2 May 2017. <http://www.musicweb-international.com/film/2004/Dec04/devils.html>.

Brody, Richard. 'The Mother and the Whore.' *New Yorker* 18 Jan. 2016: 12. Print.

Buck, Paul, *Performance: A Biography of the Classic Sixties Masterpiece*, London: Omnibus, 2012.

Cooper, Ian, *Devil's Advocates: Witchfinder General*, Leighton Buzzard: Auteur, 2011.

Crouse, Richard, *Raising Hell: Ken Russell and the Unmaking of The Devils*, Toronto: ECW, 2012.

Cutrara, Daniel S., *Wicked Cinema: Sex and Religion on Screen*, Austin: University of Texas Press, 2014.

Dargis, Manohla. "'The Passion' Minus 6 Minutes of Gore.' *The New York Times*. The New York Times Company, 14 Mar. 2005. Web. 23 Nov. 2017. <http://www.nytimes.com/2005/03/14/movies/the-passion-minus-6-minutes-of-gore.html>.

Dee, Darryl. 'Possession in the Grand Siècle: The Devils.' *Fiction and Film for French Historians*. University at Buffalo, Nov. 2012. Web. 24 Apr. 2017. <http://h-france.net/fffh/classics/possession-in-the-grand-siecle-the-devils/>.

Denby, David. 'Nailed.' *New Yorker* 1 Mar. 2004: n. pag. Print.

'The Devils.' *British Board of Film Classification*. BBFC, n.d. Web. 3 May 2017. <http://www.bbfc.co.uk/case-studies/devils>.

Flanagan, Kevin M. (ed.), *Ken Russell: Re-Viewing England's Last Mannerist*, Plymouth: Scarecrow Press, 2009.

Forcen, Fernando Espi, *Monsters, Demons and Psychopaths: Psychiatry and Horror Film*, Boca Raton: CRC Press, 2016.

Godawa, Brian, *Hollywood Worldviews*, Downers Grove: IVP Books, 2009.

Gomez, Joseph, *Ken Russell: The Adaptor As Creator*, London: Muller, 1976.

Grant, Barry Keith, 'The Body Politic: Ken Russell in the 1980s' in Flanagan, Kevin M. (ed.), *Ken Russell: Re-Viewing England's Last Mannerist*, Plymouth: Scarecrow Press, 2009.

Greene, Graham, *Brighton Rock*, New York: Viking Press, 1938.

Greene, Naomi, *Pier Paolo Pasolini: Cinema as Heresy*, Princeton: Princeton University Press, 1990.

Halliwell, Leslie, *Halliwell's Film Guide* (5th ed.), London: Paladin, 1986.

Hill, John. "'Blurring the lines between fact and fiction': Ken Russell, the BBC and 'Television Biography'.' *Journal of British Cinema and Television*. Edinburgh University Press, Sept. 2015. Web. 2 May 2017. <http://dx.doi.org/10.3366/jbctv.2015.0280>.

Huxley, Aldous, *Grey Eminence*, London: Chatto and Windus, 1941.

———, *The Devils of Loudun*, London: Chatto and Windus, 1952.

Iwaszkiewicz, Jarosław, *Nowa miłość i inne opowiadania*, Warsaw: Czytelnik, 1946.

Keefe, Robert John. 'The Devils of Loudun.' *Portico*. Pourover Press, 2005. Web. 2 May 2017. <http://www.portifex.com/ReadingMatter/DevilsLoudun.htm>.

Kerekes, David and Slater, David, *See No Evil: Banned Films and Video Controversy*, Manchester: Headpress, 2000.

────── and ──────, *Killing for Culture: From Edison to Isis: A New History of Death on Film*, London: Headpress, 2016.

Kermode, Mark. 'The Devil Himself.' *Video Watchdog* 35 (1996): 55. Print.

Lanza, Joseph, *Phallic Frenzy: Ken Russell and His Films*, Chicago: Chicago Review Press, 2007.

Maslin, Janet. "Film Festival; 'Under Satan's Sun,' On Faith and its Testing". *New York Times* 3 Oct. 1987: n. pag. Print.

Maslow, Abraham H., *The Farther Reaches of Human Nature*, New York: Viking Press, 1971.

Medori, Henri, *Les rois de France: La monarchie de Hugues Capet à Louis XVI (987 à 1792)*, Vichy: Éditions Aedis, 2013.

Mitchell, Jolyon, 'Filming the Ends of Martyrdom' in Janes, Dominic and Houen, Alex (eds), *Martyrdom and Terrorism: Pre-Modern to Contemporary Perspectives*, Oxford: Oxford University Press, 2014.

Muir, John Kenneth, 'As the (White) Worm Turns: Ken Russell as God and Devil of Rubber-Reality Horror Cinema' in Flanagan, Kevin M. (ed.), *Ken Russell: Re-Viewing England's Last Mannerist*, Plymouth: Scarecrow Press, 2009.

Nakahara, Tamao, 'Barred Nuns: Italian Exploitation Films' in Mathijs, Ernest and Mendik, Xavier (eds), *Alternative Europe: Eurotrash and Exploitation Cinema Since 1945*, London: Wallflower Press, 2004.

Olney, Ian, *Euro Horror: Classic European Horror Cinema in Contemporary American Culture*, Bloomington: Indiana University Press, 2013.

Palahniuk, Chuck, *Damned*, London: Vintage, 2011.

Peake, Tony, *Derek Jarman: A Biography*, Minneapolis: University of Minnesota Press, 2011.

Phillips, Gene D. 'An Interview with Ken Russell.' *Film Comment* 6.3 (1970): n. pag. Print.

Rabin, Nathan, *My Year of Flops*, New York: Scribner, 2010.

Robertson, James C., *The Hidden Cinema: British Film Censorship in Action, 1913-1975*, London: Routledge, 1989.

Rose, James, *Devil's Advocates: The Texas Chain Saw Massacre*, Leighton Buzzard: Auteur, 2013.

Rosenbaum, Jonathan. 'The Way We Are.' *Chicago Reader*. STM Reader, 21 Jan. 1999. Web. 20 June 2017. <https://www.chicagoreader.com/chicago/the-way-we-are/Content?oid=898239>.

Russell, Ken, *A British Picture: An Autobiography*, London: Heinemann, 1989.

Sanders, Ed, *The Family: The Story of Charles Manson's Dune Buggy Attack Battalion*, New York: E. P. Dutton, 1971.

Surin, Jean-Joseph, *Science expérimentale des choses de l'autre vie acquise en la possession des Ursulines de Loudun*, Grenoble: Jérôme Millon, 1993.

'The Texas Chain Saw Massacre.' *British Board of Film Classification*. BBFC, n.d. Web. 16 July 2018. <http://www.bbfc.co.uk/case-studies/texas-chain-saw-massacre>.

Townsend, Andy. 'Mother Joan of the Angels.' *Second Run DVD*. Second Run, 2005. Web. 21 June 2017. <http://www.secondrundvd.com/release_more_mjota>.

Trevelyan, John, *What the Censor Saw*, London: Michael Joseph, 1973.

Waddell, Calum. 'A Serbian Film.' *Total Sci-Fi*. Titan Magazines, 2 June 2010. Web. 20 June 2017. <https://web.archive.org/web/20101220045455/http://totalscifionline.com:80/reviews/5082-a-serbian-film>.

Wanyon. Comment on 'Ken Russel's [sic] The Devils uncut?' *The Cinehound Forum*. N.p., 29 July 2010. Web. 13 June 2017. <http://s9.zetaboards.com/the_cinehound_forum/topic/782550/1/>.

Whiting, John, *The Devils*, London: Heinemann, 1961.

Wistrich, Enid, *I Don't Mind the Sex, It's the Violence*, London: Marion Boyars, 1978.

Wright, Melanie J., *Religion and Film: An Introduction*, London: I. B. Tauris, 2007.

CPSIA information can be obtained
at www.ICGtesting.com
Printed in the USA
LVHW081056080519
617069LV00004B/5/P